Family Therapy with Muslims

Family Therapy with Muslims is the first guide for mental health professionals who work with Muslims in the family therapy setting. The book opens with a section defining the similarities across Muslim cultures, the effects of postcolonialism on Muslims, and typical Muslim family dynamics. The author then devotes a chapter to different models of family therapy and how they can specifically be applied to working with Muslim families. Case studies throughout the book involve families of many different backgrounds living in the West—including both immigrant and second-generation families—and will give professionals concrete tools to work with clients of their own.

Manijeh Daneshpour, PhD, LMFT, is a professor in the department of couple and family therapy at Alliant International University in Irvine, California, and a licensed marriage and family therapist with 20 years of academic and clinical experience. Dr. Daneshpour's main areas of research, publications, and presentations have been centered on issues of multiculturalism, social justice, third wave feminism, premarital and marital relationships, and Muslim family dynamics. She has studied Muslim families not as a religious group, but as individuals, members of family units, and a distinct group within their own societal context.

Family Therapy with Muslims

Manijeh Daneshpour

Routledge
Taylor & Francis Group
NEW YORK AND LONDON

First published 2017
by Routledge
711 Third Avenue, New York, NY 10017

and by Routledge
2 Park Square, Milton Park, Abingdon, Oxon, OX14 4RN

Routledge is an imprint of the Taylor & Francis Group, an informa business

Library of Congress Cataloging-in-Publication Data
Names: Daneshpour, Manijeh, author.
Title: Family therapy with Muslims / by Manijeh Daneshpour.
Description: New York, NY : Routledge, 2016. | Includes bibliographical references and index.
Identifiers: LCCN 2016007263 | ISBN 9781138947962 (hbk : alk. paper) | ISBN 9781138947979 (pbk. : alk. paper) | ISBN 9781315669762 (ebook)
Subjects: LCSH: Family psychotherapy. | Muslims. | Cross-cultural counseling.
Classification: LCC RC488.5 D334 2016 | DDC 616.89/156088297–dc23
LC record available at https://lccn.loc.gov/2016007263

ISBN: 978-1-138-94796-2 (hbk)
ISBN: 978-1-138-94797-9 (pbk)
ISBN: 978-1-315-66976-2 (ebk)

Typeset in ITC Legacy Serif
by Apex CoVantage, LLC

CONTENTS

ACKNOWLEDGMENTS

As a systemic thinker, I have long been a believer that no one walks alone on the journey of life or becomes anything useful without unconditional emotional support alternating with the occasional emotional challenges. Therefore, I need to extend great gratitude to those who inspired me, supported me, walked beside me, and continuously helped me along this wavering path. I must convey equal appreciation to those who lacked faith in me and doubted my ability to thrive and succeed. Their challenges allowed my personal growth and ability to mix the bitterness of failures and disappointments with the sweet taste of success and contentment. They taught me to recognize that success is temporary if we don't work consistently to improve our abilities. Over the years, my students and clients have taught me more than any professional by simply believing in my ability to teach and guide them whilst appreciating my continual, positive approach to life and all that it throws our way.

My most heartfelt gratitude goes to my parents and siblings for their strong encouragement and unconditional love. They have always been a steadfast source of support and have been constant and consistent in their dependability—I am greatly indebted to them. I also thank my husband, Amir, with whom I have had the pleasure of feeling loved in the purest form. Over the years, he has taught me much about myself and the mysterious ways that love can make a difference in our view of life's challenges. A great deal of what I have learned over the years came as the result of being a mother to two wonderful and delightful children, Hoda and Neda. In their own ways they have inspired me and subconsciously contributed a tremendous amount to how I perceive myself as a loving mother and competent professional woman. It would not be possible to be who I am without their support and love.

This list of acknowledgments can only capture a small fraction of the people who have supported me over the years, but a special thanks goes to Iman for buying books and sending me articles about this topic, for engaging in meaningful conversations about the content of this book, and for incessantly challenging my perceptions of Muslim families. I also need to thank my graduate student Mi Ki for being readily available to help me with any of my tasks. The most special and deepest thanks go to my Middle Eastern clients who made the creation of this book possible. Their contributions to this book were vital, but the inevitable mistakes or misrepresentation are very much my own.

Further, all the founders of the family therapy models covered in this book have a very special place in my heart because, without these models, I would not have been able to provide vigorous and dynamic family therapy to so many families over the years.

And lastly, I am deeply indebted to everyone who has provided fuel to my burning passion and powerful conviction to be an advocate for social justice and advocacy work. I can only hope to be true to myself and always remember to promote a humanistic and equitable approach to life and living.

A FEW WORDS ABOUT ME

Although an Iranian native, I have lived in the West for the entirety of my adult life and have received all my academic education in the United States. However, I have been very closely and deeply connected to Eastern cultural dynamics and have grown to appreciate the very diverse richness of the Eastern backdrop, particularly as it is juxtaposed with my Western way of life on a daily basis. I have been trained as a marriage and family therapist and provided numerous hours of couple and family therapy to European Americans and countless therapy sessions to Eastern families, including Muslims. As an academician, I have taught various courses in family therapy theories and have supervised numerous European and Eastern American therapists alike. I have trained Western family therapists to provide culturally sensitive couple and family therapy to Muslim families and have trained Eastern international students to provide therapy relevant to the current Western cultural context. Although I served as somewhat of an ambassador between the Western and Eastern therapy mindset, much of my research efforts and publications have been centered on Muslim family dynamics—not as a religious group but as a cultural group—an arena in which I have grown both comfortable and quite familiar.

Drawing from my experiences over the years, I have found Muslim families, like any other minority group, to be both intricately unique and simplistically typical in so many ways. As Easterners in general, we operate based on many collectivistic cultural values first, while as Muslims in particular we use a mixture of local cultural rituals and Islamic ideologies as a way of life second. Indeed, I am very much a realist and pragmatist in my view of Islamic cultures and family dynamics. As a researcher, I am duly conscious that Muslim families deal with the same issues as other cultural groups. However, our culturally based Islamic values often prevent us from identifying, discussing, and delving into solutions for these shared struggles that many other Eastern, non-Muslim cultural groups have admitted to and attempted to resolve before we were even willing to admit them. My Western and Eastern colleagues alike have often confronted me in regards to where I stand with respect to these cultural and religious issues. On the one hand, I wear *hijab*, which cross-culturally represents a deep connection to Islam as a religion. On the other, I wear this headpiece as a representation of my sociopolitical agenda, which attempts to challenge both the Eastern and Western notion of how an educated, open-minded, and modern woman should appear physically.

My sociopolitical, religious, clinical, and academic backgrounds are deep foundations for the urgency to write this book to share my professional knowledge, experience, and expertise. This book is my absolute unpretentious attempt to cover several applicable family therapy theories and the clinical implications for applying them while working with Muslim families living in both Muslim- and non-Muslim-dominated countries globally. I am painfully aware that this is indeed a very ambitious undertaking, particularly given all the differences in behaviors ranging in scope from the single-family interaction, the shared community sphere, and essentially the societal normative perspective. Thankfully, the goal is not to explain every behavior and interaction; rather, it is to give readers an overall understanding of how to use family therapy theories in working with Muslim families as individuals, as members of family units, and as groups within their societal context. A myriad of generalizations will be made in an effort to make room for more specific ways of thinking for mental health professionals working with Muslim families globally. Thus, these general assumptions about family interactions are made only to make professionals be less assuming and more open to a family's way of defining their own connections. This book, simply put, is an effort to reintroduce some Western family therapy models to mental health practitioners who plan to work with this population as they have shown great usefulness and applicability in my own work with Muslim families over the past 20 years.

INTRODUCTION

Today there are more than 50 Muslim states with distinct cultural and ecological contexts. There are high-populated countries like Indonesia, Nigeria, Bangladesh, and Pakistan and less populated countries like Bahrain and Kuwait. Some have strong and effective government systems, such as Saudi Arabia, Qatar, and United Arab Emirates, and some are struggling to exist, like Bosnia, Somalia, and Syria. There are countries with very weak economies, like Mali and Bangladesh, and there are countries with strong economies and a wealth of natural resources, such as Saudi Arabia, Iran, Turkmenistan, and Libya. Other countries like the United Arab Emirates and Malaysia have used industrialization to build successful economies. Some Muslim countries are compromised of mostly one ethnic group, such as most Arab countries, while others include several different ethnic groups with different languages and cultural backgrounds, as in Iran. There are all kinds of sociopolitical, economic, and ideological representations in these states. While there are secular countries like the United Arab Emirates or Indonesia, countries like the Islamic Republic of Iran and Saudi Arabia have based their governments on religious ideology. There are monarchies in Malaysia, Nigeria, and Brunei and democracies in Indonesia, Turkey, Pakistan, Bangladesh, and Malaysia.

Despite this diversity among Muslim states, the most apparent common thread is the religion of Islam as a source of identity and an imperative influence on all aspects of life including cultural and relational patterns for Muslim families. It is important to recognize that even though cultural context and religious orientation cannot always explain a Muslim family's behavior, and sometimes even experiences of a person from a particular culture cannot be explained by any specific cultural values that one has been taught but the recognition of irrelevance can come in the context of knowledge. This means that we need to have an understanding of the cultural context in which Muslim families live in order to recognize whether and to what degree cultural experiences pertain to one's personality, experiences, and problems.

Further, we need to understand how normal behavior is defined by a specific cultural context in order to make sense of family functioning. Normal psychological functioning is usually defined as the behavior that is very common. However, this definition has a bias because most Westerners control the institutional powers, and, therefore, their behavioral patterns are considered normal not only for them but for anyone residing within their cultural context and also other cultures (Sue & Sue, 2013). Often what is considered to be normal or mentally healthy is that which fits within the boundaries of Western social contexts. However, social norms vary; what is considered mentally healthy varies with culture, education, age, and, most of the time, gender.

Does a female college student have psychological problems if at age 27 she still lives with her parents because she is not married? Should her friends think that she has a problem with individuation? What if she has a hard time socializing with the opposite sex in front of her parents and relatives but feels very comfortable talking and spending time with men at her workplace and school? Is the problem that she has multiple personality or highly unpredictable behavior? We might judge her behavior differently if we knew if she was a Westerner or a Muslim immigrant from a very traditional Muslim family.

Therefore, assessing whether a behavior is pathological most often depends on the context in which the behavior takes place. A person who believes that a given behavior is either normal/psychologically healthy or abnormal/psychologically unhealthy, without considering the social context, will have a hard time trying to justify many variations in behavior across cultures and ecological contexts (Uba, 2003).

If we allow the definition of 'normal' to be dictated by the dominant social norms of the Western culture, using the *Diagnostic and Statistical Manual* to diagnose individuals with mental health disorders, we imply that mental health is defined by the social norms of the Western culture, which means whatever behaviors they do or approve are mentally healthy and whatever they do not do or disapprove are mentally unhealthy. Therefore, a culturally sensitive definition of 'normal' must be relativistic and should consider the ecological contexts and their cultural values and viewpoints.

Cultural Values and Viewpoints

It is important to have an understanding and appreciation of Muslim family values and viewpoints because of the implications of these beliefs for their behaviors. Certainly, there are differences among Muslim families just as there are among members of other groups. Muslim families hold traditional Islamic and cultural values to varying degrees. It is very possible that not all Muslim families adhere to all these values. Furthermore, the values of some Muslim families might be relatively traditional whereas the values of other Muslim families might be so typically 'Western' that it would be difficult to distinguish their values from those of the so-called average Westerner. In between these poles would be innumerable variations.

It is not even completely accurate to define the extremes of the values continuum as traditional Muslim family ideals versus Western ideals. It is even disingenuous to label one extreme as 'traditional Muslim family values' when even the most traditional Muslim family might hold Islamic beliefs that are not traditional. Muslim family principles and cultures evolve, and cultures of today are not the same as traditional cultures of centuries ago. At the other end of the continuum, it is also misleading to talk about 'Western values' as if they were homogenous, clearly defined, static, and synonymous with middle-class, Euro-American attitudes and opinions. Because other than individual differences, there are numerous social class, gender, and regional differences embedded in Western values. In addition, many Western values are not necessarily the opposite of Muslim family values; therefore, it is inaccurate to put these sets of Western and Muslim family values at opposite ends of a continuum.

Moreover, an additive model would not accurately reflect how Muslim families synthesize Islamic and Western values and viewpoints. Individuals do not simply combine traditional Islamic and Western values. Instead, the very blending and balancing of values within different personal and social contexts is a dynamic and amalgamated process. Muslim families will vary in the synthesis of their own experiences and Western culture as a function of their intelligence, education, gender, exposure to Islamic culture, and many other factors including the extent of colonization, years of independence, and their current government's connection to the West. Nonetheless, some benefits can be derived from understanding traditional Islamic beliefs as long as these beliefs create a context for Muslim family values.

Book Organization

This book has been divided in two parts. In part 1, I cover important religious and cultural background information regarding Islam and Muslim families. In part 2, I cover seven family therapy models that I have found beneficial in working with Muslim families while residing both in the Middle East and the US. Chapter 1 covers Muslim beliefs and gives non-Muslim mental health professionals a very basic and general overview of Muslims' spiritual values. Chapter 2 covers family dynamics and relational patterns for 23 distinct Muslim states, attempting to show similarities and differences in how family relationships are defined in these countries. Chapter 3 covers the impact of centuries of colonization on Muslim families' perception of themselves and their relationships with each other and the West. Chapter 4 attempts to cover the politics of Muslim cultures' gender dynamics and how this topic has been analyzed and perceived from Western viewpoints.

In part 2, chapter 5 covers family assessment concepts and general information regarding how to use family therapy concepts in working with Muslim families. Chapter 6 covers structural family therapy concepts and a case example to show how this model can be used in working with Muslim families. Chapter 7 covers Bowenian family therapy and the usefulness of this model in working with Muslim families even though the concepts of individuation and differentiation may seem to have less relevance in working with Easterners based on their collectivistic cultural backgrounds. A case example shows how this model can be used effectively and appropriately. Chapter 8 covers the experiential family therapy of Karl Whitaker and Virginia Satir because of the humanistic foundation of this model and its applicability in clinical work with Muslim families. A case example using Satir's communication and self-esteem building model shows how to use this approach appropriately. Chapter 9 covers narrative family therapy concepts and the importance of the use of language and metaphors in working with Muslim families. A clinical case example shows the usefulness of narrative therapy in working with this population. Chapter 10 covers contextual family therapy, which is a comprehensive approach to family pathology using relational ethics. A case example shows the inclusive nature of this model in working with Muslim families. Chapter 11 covers feminist family therapy to show the usefulness of a gender-based model in working with Muslim families. The clinical case example reveals how this can be done. Chapter 12 covers post-modern family therapy and the use of 'mini-narratives' and the meaning families assign to their experiences to help with their family functioning. A case example shows the powerful clinical nature of this perspective.

Thus, my main goal is to have a theory-based practical guide for clinicians working with Muslim families while keeping original family therapy models alive and relevant in this age of growing superficial evidence-based models and empty claims for clinical effectiveness. I also wanted to tell the story of several Muslim families to highlight their unique as well as typical family dilemmas. I hope readers across the globe find this book useful, timely, and practical.

REFERENCES

Sue, D.W., & Sue, D. (2013). *Counseling the culturally diverse: Theory and practice* (6th ed.). New York: John Wiley & Sons.

Uba, L. (2003). *Asian Americans: Personality patterns, identity, and mental health.* New York: Guilford.

Part I

Muslim Spiritual, Social, Family, and Political History

Chapter 1

MUSLIM BELIEFS

Related group bonds tie individuals in any society together. Families have the strongest societal bonds and are the foundation of all human societies, including Muslims. Roughly one out of five individual across the globe is Muslim and belongs to a family (Berkley Center for Religion, Peace, and Affairs, 2013), but even in this age of global interconnection with extensive technological advances connecting all societies together most Westerners with Christian upbringings know little about Islam and Muslim families. This chapter will discuss basic principles of the religion of Islam to familiarize mental health professionals mostly from Western cultural backgrounds with the central Muslim beliefs. It is important to note that while many Muslims may not practice their religion, culturally they may operate their daily lives based on these principles either consciously or consciously.

Islam and Muslims

Islam is a monotheistic and Abrahamic religion communicated through the Quran. Muslims believe that the entire Quran is authentic words of God. Muslims also believe that Mohammed is the last prophet of God, and followers of Islam respect and regard his teachings, the Sunnah and Hadith, as exemplary and the best guidance for Muslims' conduct and mannerisms. Islam is believed to have the same messages that were revealed many times before through Abraham, Moses, and Jesus. Muslims assert that the earlier messages and revelations from God through other prophets before Mohammed have been partly misinterpreted or changed over time (Peters, 2003). However, the Quran is considered unchanged without any alterations and is believed to be the final revelation of God (Esposito, 2010). Five pillars of Islam that cover essential acts of worship and the primary religious concepts and practices touch on essentially all aspects of life and society (Esposito, 2010).

The two major denominations in Islam are Sunni (80%–90% and Shia 10%–20%). Indonesia, with about 13% of its population Muslim, is the largest Muslim-majority country. It is estimated that about 25% of Muslims live in South Asia, 20% live in the Middle East, and 15% live in sub-Saharan Africa (Berkley Center for Religion, Peace, and Affairs, 2013). Considerable minorities also live in China, Russia, and the Americas, and many immigrants and converts live in different countries across the globe. In essence, after Christianity, Islam is considered to be the second largest religion; it has 1.57 billion followers comprising 23% of the world's population (Berkley Center for Religion, Peace, and Affairs, 2013; Miller, 2009).

MUSLIM BELIEF SYSTEM

God/Allah

Islam's most primary and basic concept is monotheism. Muslims renounce the Christian principle of the trinity and the holiness of Jesus as the son of God and consider it as polytheism. In Islam, God's relation to humans is personal; God is always available for a person in need, and there is no need for intermediaries such as clergy to intercept the relationship between human and God. 'Allah' is the genderless word that Muslims and anyone who speaks Arabic, including Jews and Christians, use to refer to God, while non-Arabic-speaking Muslims use different names like 'Tanrı' in Turkish or 'Khodā' in Farsi.

Angels

The Arabic word for angel means 'Messenger,' and belief in angels is a fundamental concept in Islam. According to the Quran, angels worship God in complete submission and do not possess their own free will. Angels' responsibilities include communicating revelations from God to his prophets, praising God, taking the soul at the time of a person's death, and recording every person's actions to be evaluated at the Day of Judgment (Esposito, 2010).

Believing in a Day of Judgment

Belief in the Day of Judgment is imperative for Muslims. They believe God has predetermined the time for human resurrection but that the time is unknown to us. The details regarding events before and during the Day of Judgment are explained in the Quran, and the Hadith, and also by many Muslim scholars. Muslims believe that on the Day of Judgment, all mankind's good and bad deeds will be judged by God.

Predestination

Islamic belief in predestination, or celestial preordainment, indicates that God is in control of everything before it happens and has full knowledge of events even before they occur. Therefore, for Muslims, everything that happens, good or bad, has been predetermined, and nothing transpires without God's permission (Esposito, 2002). However, Muslim scholars state that, even though events are predetermined, humans have free will, can always choose between right and wrong, and are accountable and liable for all actions (Esposito, 2002).

Five Pillars

The Pillars of Islam are five basic acts considered to be essential for every Muslim believer. In Islamic teaching and the Quran, these five pillars are considered the main framework for reverence and indicate a devotion to the Islamic principles. These are: the shahadah (creed); salat (daily prayers); zakat (almsgiving); sawm (fasting during Ramadan); and hajj (the pilgrimage to Mecca). The Shia and Sunni who are the largest denominations in Islam agree on the fundamental elements for performing these acts (Esposito, 2004).

Shahadah

The shahadah is the rudimentary principle of Islam and must be narrated under oath stating: "I attest there are no divinities other than

God alone and Muhammad is the Messenger of God." The shahadah is the basic tribute, and Muslims must repeat it in all their daily prayer. Non-Muslims who wish to convert to Islam must recite this statement as well (Esposito, 2004).

Salat

Formal prayers, called Ṣalāt, are to be performed five times a day. Salat is supposed to connect humans to God and is a form of sequestered communication with him expressing gratitude and devotion. Salat is obligatory for all Muslims, but there may be flexibility in details contingent on specific situations. Regardless of the individual's native language, salat must be narrated in Arabic because it contains verses from the Quran (Kobeisy, 2004).

Zakat

'Zakāt' is giving away part of personal wealth to help the poor or needy. Since wealth is given to human from God, wealthier individuals are supposed to take care of those in need in their communities. According to irinnews.org, a conservative estimate of the zakat given annually is 15 times more than global charitable aid contributions altogether (2013). It is encouraged both by the Quran and the Hadith for Muslims to contribute more resources voluntarily, which is called sadagah (Quran).

Sawm

Restraining from eating and drinking (among other things) from dawn to dusk during the month of Ramadan is obligatory for Muslim believers. Fasting is supposed to create a closer connection to God in order to express gratitude and dependence, repent from past sins, and also think of the needy. People who are either sick, traveling, or have other reasons for not fasting are not obligated to fast. Others can also not fast depending on their situation but need to make up for missed days later if they can (Esposito, 2004).

Hajj

The ḥajj, or pilgrimage, is performed in the city of Mecca during the Islamic month of Dhu-al-Hijjah. Muslims who are financially and physically able to afford this pilgrimage must go to Mecca at least once in their lifetime. There are specific sacraments during the performance of hajj, which includes walking seven times around the Kaaba (house of God), walking seven times between the two mounts of Safa and Marwah, and symbolically stoning Satan in Mina (Esposito, 2004).

The Presence of Fundamentalism in Islam

Islam and Christianity are both expansionist religions and seek to preach and convert nonbelievers. However, Christianity grew within a pre-existing state system (the Roman Empire) and then became a separate political power. Islam, on the other hand, started from filling a political vacuum and created a force for a new state. Therefore, the ultimate separation between church and state in Christianity does not occur in Islam.

The term 'fundamentalism' instigated in the United States based on the political movement of anti-progressive Christians desiring to combine social and political issues with Christian beliefs. Thus, it is confusing to apply the label of 'fundamentalist' to Muslims when this kind of division between matters social, political, and religious should not even exist in Islam. There are, of course, differences in how this unity between religion and politics should be put into practice, but by definition the label 'fundamentalist' does not make much sense when applied to Muslims and their belief systems.

Religious versus Cultural Practices

Islam spread rapidly because of the way it adapted itself to the pre-existing cultural practices it came into contact with. If these cultural practices were not openly in opposition to the basic tenants of Islamic practices, they were adopted into the newly Islamic culture. Over time many of these pre-Islamic cultural practices have been labeled as endorsed by Islam by traditionalist forces in these societies.

Subsequently, what is declared as part of Islamic ideology and practices is more frequently the pre-existing cultural and social traditions of these ethnic societies. For example, many of the Islamic practices of Afghans, Persians, Pashtuns, Arabs, and East Asians have more in common with cultural norms than Islamic laws. However, over time these traditions and Islamic beliefs have become so intertwined that it is hard to argue where traditional practices end and Islam begins.

MAJOR SECTS IN ISLAM: SUNNI VERSUS SHIA

The dominant branch of Islam is Sunni, and between 80% to 90% of Muslims belong to this sect. Although the split between the two main branches of Sunni and Shia was initially about who should succeed Muhammad, it later evolved to much more extensive political and philosophical dissimilarities. Since Muhammad did not have a son, the Muslim community did not know who should be the leader of the Muslim community after his death. The main group (current Sunnis) decided that the leadership (the caliphate) should pass on to someone who could best represent continuity. The Shias, on the other hand, believed that only God could determine the legitimacy of the caliphate and supported the leadership of Ali, the husband of the prophet's favorite daughter.

Over time, those who knew the prophet and remembered his sayings helped write down these oral traditions of guidance (Sunnah) that were complementary to the Quran, which became several books recognized as authoritative sources of guidance called the Hadith. For Sunnis, societal laws and regulations must be based on the Quran and the Sunnah. For Shi'ites, only the divinely appointed intermediaries that are the true caliphs or imams can show the right path.

SUFI

Over the centuries, the personal and spiritual aspects of Islam intrigued certain groups of Muslims to achieve some kinds of direct unification with God. This special interest seems to be influenced by other Eastern traditions that are also in search of enlightenment like Hindu, Buddhist, or Taoist. The Sufi traditions are seen as deviating from mainstream Islamic believes and are condemned by authoritarian Islamic powers. The contemplative struggle of the Sufis is a form of struggle against the insincere and deceptive earthly self. Sufis practices are also associated with physical forces like music and wild dancing to create visions and spiritual stimulations, which makes Sufis ostracized by those Muslims who believe that dancing, music, and celebration in general are not appropriate forms of worship in Islam.

CLINICAL IMPLICATIONS

Despite the differences in terms of how Muslim individuals identify with different sects of Islam or even how closely they practice their religion,

Islamic beliefs serve as a link connecting many different cultures and provide a shared context for understanding family life. Muslim family structure driving from Islamic ideology is primarily patriarchal, and, if it does not include the extended family directly, it is at least heavily influenced by it. Customs, traditions, and sacraments to celebrate important life cycle events often have religious foundations, which creates imperative similarities through the life cycle for both individual and family developmental tasks (Daneshpour, 1998). Therefore, it is essential for non-Muslim family therapists to become familiar with the basic tenants of Islam and incorporate their understanding in working with Muslim families.

References

Berkley Center for Religion, Peace, and World Affairs. (2013, October). *Wikipedia*. Retrieved from http://en.wikipedia.org/wiki/Berkley_Center_for_Religion,_Peace,and_World_Affairs

Daneshpour, M. (1998). Muslim families and family therapy. *Journal of Marriage and Family Therapy, 24*, 287–300. doi:10.1111/j.1752-0606.1998.tb01090.x

Esposito, J. (2002). *What everyone needs to know about Islam*. New York: Oxford University Press.

Esposito, J. (2004). *Islam: The straight path* (3rd rev. ed.). New York: Oxford University Press.

Esposito, J. (2010). *Islam: The straight path* (4th ed.). New York: Oxford University Press.

Kobeisy, A.N. (2004). *Counseling American Muslims: Understanding the faith and helping the people*. Santa Barbara, CA: Praeger Publishers.

Miller, T. (Ed.). (2009). *Mapping the global Muslim population: A report on the size and distribution of the world's Muslim population*. Retrieved from Pew Research Center website: www.pewforum.org/2009/10/07/mapping-the-global-muslim-population/

Peters, F.E. (2003). *Islam: A guide for Jews and Christians*. Princeton, NJ: Princeton University.

Chapter 2

MUSLIM COUNTRIES

The term 'Muslims' applies to members of more than 50 Islam-dominated countries worldwide because of their common ethnic origins and supposedly similar religious and some cultural values. Therefore, the classification of a multitude of groups under the single rubric of Muslims carries some potential danger. For example, important differences among groups can be overlooked. In fact, Muslim families culturally and experientially are quite diverse: they differ in cultural values and beliefs, primary language, personality syndromes, income, education, ethnic identity, and so forth. Further, subsuming separate groups under the single category of Muslims also can blind the unwary to dissimilarities among individuals and can easily create unnecessary stereotypes. In addition to interethnic differences (i.e., variations among Muslim country), there are intraethnic differences (variation within each Muslim country) in gender dynamics, generational expectations, attitude towards others, traumatic experiences due to war, national identity, and so forth that affect personality patterns, sources of stress, identity conflicts, attitudes, and the need for mental health services.

However, the majority of Muslims live in the Eastern countries, and their cultures appear to be more collectivist and authoritarian as opposed to individualistic and liberal. These cultures emphasize family integrity, harmony, interdependence, saving face, authority, and hierarchy within the collective, so family integrity, obedience, and conformity values override competition, pleasure, and self-fulfillment. Social and geographical mobility is very limited (Dwairy, 2006). People tend to live near their parents, and their behavior is regulated mostly by collective norms that are more important than an individual's attitudes. The 'self' is defined as an appendage of the collective, and an individual's identity is associated with social affiliation to the family or tribe rather than to personal qualities or achievements. Social relationships are close and cooperative and involve much hospitality and generosity (Dwairy, 2006). In order to understand some of these interethnic and intraethnic differences it is important to look into some family dynamic issues for some predominantly Muslim countries. It is important to note that only countries with some historical and familial differences have been included in this chapter.

Afghanistan

The recent history of Afghanistan has been impacted first by war with Russia, then Taliban-controlled government, and very recently war with the US. Therefore there have been many changes in terms of family relationships, gender roles, and the importance of religion and extended family interactions. Nevertheless, there are several general themes that help us understand Afghani family dynamics better. For example, family and tribal ties play an important role in shaping the identities of the Afghan people (Gerami, 2003); kinship is traced through the male line (Monsutti, 2001), and gender roles in the family are traditional. If the family is well-off, men are expected to be the family's breadwinners and work outside the home while women are expected to stay at home to run the household. Gender role designation is stricter in urban areas than in rural parts of the country (Cogswell & Gerami, 2003). A woman's actions influence the honor of her male relatives (Gerami, 2003). Because any female's indiscretion could lower the status of her male relatives, women's interactions, especially in the public sphere, are closely monitored. Women may have less authority in society, but they have considerable authority in matters concerning the home (Daeg de Mott, 1998a).

A typical household in Afghanistan includes multiple generations (Monsutti, 2001). Newlyweds move into the husband's family home and continue to live there as they raise their children. When the oldest male in a family passes away, his sons can choose to stay in the family home or divide up the family assets and become the heads of separate households. Sons may also choose to move from the family household before the death of their father.

Marriage is understood to be an obligation in Afghan culture (Monsutti, 2001). A marriage contract is arranged between the families of a bride and groom. Afghanis typically marry within their tribal lineage (Gerami, 2003). Divorce is rare and socially looked down upon (Monsutti, 2001). While it is legal for a man to take up to four wives as long as he can care for each equally, working and middle-class families rarely can afford to have more than one wife.

Children are cherished members of Afghani families (Daeg de Mott, 1998a). Female family members assist mothers in childcare duties (Monsutti, 2001). The birth of a son increases the status of the mother and is preferred over the birth of a daughter (Cogswell & Gerami, 2003). Afghani parents have been known to be very affectionate towards their children, but children are not given any extra attention when they cry or are hurt (Monsutti, 2001). Children are expected to grow up quickly (Cogswell & Gerami, 2003). Early in life, boys are expected to show hospitality towards guests. Girls are expected to help their mothers around the house (Monsutti, 2001) and to care for younger siblings (Cogswell & Gerami, 2003). Children are raised to respect their elders, to be independent and self-confident (Monsutti, 2001). Male circumcision around age seven is a significant rite of passage for young boys (Daeg de Mott, 1998a).

Algeria

Families operate in a tightly knit community (Abed-Kotob, 1998a). The family structure consist of the parents, paternal grandparents, unmarried children, and married children and their families as well as widowed or divorced females from extended families and their children (Stanford, 2001a). Algerian couples typically have a higher number of children (Stanford, 2001a). Within families with stronger Arabic influence, loyalty to the family is very important as affiliations are traditionally based on blood relations (Stanford, 2001a); however, due to the war, many extended family units were broken, and many also started to build loyalties with other people who bonded with them during the trying times (Abed-Kotob, 1998a). Since the country's independence, it is more common to have only nuclear families within the household (Stanford, 2001a), although they keep close ties with their extended families (Issitt, 2008a).

Traditionally, women had to seek the permission of their fathers or husbands before they were able to engage in various activities or work outside the home (Stanford, 2001a). However, during the war, women gained more status within society through their contributions, and they became more expressive in order to maintain their status in modern society (Abed-Kotob, 1998a). In modern times, it is still common for rural women to fulfill traditional roles while those in urban areas are more active outside the household (Issitt, 2008a).

Men and women rarely socialize together, and gender separation is common during gatherings (Abed-Kotob, 1998a). Since dating is also not allowed (Abed-Kotob, 1998a), marriages are typically arranged by the parents or a professional matchmaker (Abed-Kotob, 1998a; Stanford, 2001a). Although it is uncommon, polygamy is allowed whereby husbands are allowed to have up to four wives legally (Issitt, 2008a; Stanford, 2001a). The right to divorce solely belongs to the husband (Stanford, 2001a).

Children are raised by the entire family living in the same household (Abed-Kotob, 1998a), and women are the primary caregivers to the children (Abed-Kotob, 1998a; Stanford, 2001a). Gender roles are reinforced in the families whereby girls are taught to be obedient and attend to the boys' needs and domestic duties. On the other hand, boys are allowed to have more social freedom (Stanford, 2001a). Although this trend is diminishing, men are typically given more opportunities for education compared to women (Stanford, 2001a).

Bangladesh

The most common domestic unit is the patrilineally related extended family (Lodrick, 1998a). This unit is significant in terms of economic endeavor, with jointly held property and household activities under the father's authority (Lodrick, 1998a). The household consists of the nuclear family with unmarried children and married sons and their families as well as grandparents and patrilineally related brothers, cousins, nieces, and nephews (Harris, 2001). Although married sons remain under their father's authority while their wives remain under the mother-in-law's, the sons may build a separate house for their own nuclear families (Mesbah & Huda, 2008). In rural areas, three or four houses face each other in a square courtyard, and common tasks and food supplies are shared among the family members (Harris, 2001). The death of the father usually marks the separation of the sons from this united household (Mesbah & Huda, 2008).

Marriage normally takes place when the parents, especially the father, decide the child should be married (Harris, 2001). It is common for parents to make arrangements for their children to wed a member of a family of similar religious, economic, and education background (Harris, 2001). Children are allowed to review the choices, rule out unacceptable candidates, and select the most suitable spouse (Harris, 2001). Some families may also adopt the Hindu custom of providing a dowry for their daughter's wedding (Lodrick, 1998a), and the marriage arrangement between the two families becomes official upon an agreement with the dowry and gift arrangements (Harris, 2001). However, the practice of dowry is no longer prevalent among the educated (Harris, 2001).

In child-rearing, most women return to their natal homes to give birth (Harris, 2001). The husbands are informed thereafter and visit the newborn five or seven days after birth; this is usually followed by a feast and various rituals (Harris, 2001). The newborns are breast fed and constantly remain with their mothers, sisters, or other women in the household, who are considered primary child caregivers (Harris, 2001). Children are raised to be respectful and follow orders of those who are older than them (Harris, 2001). As children are raised within the extended family, they are taught that family needs precede individual desires (Harris, 2001). Children begin school at five or six years of age, and schooling typically drops off as they go higher in grades and become more productive within the household based on the chores for different genders (Harris, 2001). Children from families with higher socioeconomic status have a much greater chance to get a higher education, and higher statuses are accorded to those with university or professional qualifications (Harris, 2001).

In poorer families, since daughters are considered transitory family members who will be married off with a dowry, for economic reasons, parents invest in their sons, who will be the heirs and providers, over their daughters (Mesbah & Huda, 2008). Instead of going to school, daughters are usually expected to assist in domestic chores at home (Mesbah & Huda, 2008). In general, discrimination against females is against the law (Mesbah & Huda, 2008); however, females remain subordinate to men as they continue to have access limitations in the workplace, and gender segregation remains even among modernized groups (Lodrick, 1998a).

Egypt

The family remains as the central and most important aspect of Egyptian life (Sherif, 2003). Identification with family is an important primary social marker supported by linguistics and social class divisions (Sherif, 2003).

Most Egyptian households consist of nuclear families instead of extended families (Mwaniki, 1998). The common trend of households with extended families has changed due to urbanization and migration in search of employment (Mwaniki, 1998). Patriarchal authority rules over the family and is to be obeyed (Hopkins & Saad, 2001). There is a clear distinction between the gender roles whereby fathers are expected to become the head of the family and provide financially for the household while, on the other hand, mothers are the primary caregivers who also manage domestic household responsibilities (Mwaniki, 1998). Males and females are socialized with gender expectations within the family, and to prepare for their future roles as wife and mother, females are generally expected to take on more household chores and have less mobility outside the home (Assaad, Levision, & Zibani, 2005; Mensch, Ibrahim, Lee, & El-Gibably, 2003; as cited in Rowe & Rizzo, 2008). Males have more freedom to venture out of the home and be involved in communities to prepare them as future providers and the head of a family (Mensch et al., 2003). This gender complementarity forms an integral part of the social structure in Egypt (Sherif, 2003).

Extensive kin ties are maintained in Egyptian households through frequent family gatherings even after married children establish their own nuclear families (Hopkins & Saad, 2001). Married sons seek to live near their parents, and those who are not able to afford to live on their own move in with their parents (Mwaniki, 1998). It is common for families to live very close to each other or even in the same apartment building (Sherif, 2003). Single children of any age, including unmarried, divorced, or widowed extended family members, live with their families, especially when their parents are still alive (Sherif, 2003). Single-person households are stigmatized and rare (Sherif, 2003). Households may also include work apprentices or assistants who are not related to the family as upper-middle-class or upper-class families employ domestic servants from their natal villages (Sherif, 2003).

Every Egyptian is expected to get married and procreate to continue the family lineage (Mwaniki, 1998). Since premarital sex is rare, the pressure to marry is high (Hopkins & Saad, 2001). Currently, hierarchical marriage has been gradually replaced by companionate marriage, especially among the urban middle class (Hopkins & Saad, 2001). Although Egyptians may choose who they marry, many parties including family members and matchmakers are involved in the selection process (Hopkins & Saad, 2001). It is common for marriage partners to be similar in age and level of education (Hopkins & Saad, 2001). Marriages between cousins are also common (Hopkins & Saad, 2001). For Muslim Egyptian marriages, the betrothal that takes place before a marriage is legalized allows the couples to spend chaperoned time together and get to know each other better. The family members of the bride and groom will also start spending more time with their prospective new family members (Sherif, 2003).

After marriage, females retain their family names and preserve close ties to their natal families and are expected to return to their natal home should they be separated from their husbands (Sherif, 2003). Divorce is allowed; however, families often attempt to reconcile the couple (Hopkins & Saad, 2001). With the reform of child custody laws, mothers generally retain custody of young children until they are 15 years of age, and this can remain so unless the child decides to choose to live with the father (Hopkins & Saad, 2001).

Childcare is mainly the women's responsibility, with extended families playing an active role in a child's upbringing (Hopkins & Saad, 2001). Children from both genders are treated equally; however, there is a preference for at least one male in the family in order to provide continuity to the family lineage (Hopkins & Saad, 2001). Children are taught to respect their parents and adults older than them (Mwaniki, 1998). Education is also highly valued in Egyptian society, where children are educated as much as possible (Hopkins & Saad, 2001). In poorer families, males are expected to work at an early age instead of attending school (Mwaniki, 1998).

Indonesia

"Indonesians value family closeness, loyalty, obligation and respect" (Davis, Limansubroto, Piercy, & Soekandar, 2005). Strong connections are maintained within the family circle as well as the surrounding community such as the clan, village, mosque, or workplace (Hus & Jarchow,

2008). Although there are differences in kinship among different ethnicities, the household typically consist of the nuclear family, grandparents, unmarried relatives, and servants (Abalahin, 1998). Patrilineal descent is the most common kinship grouping, although there are also different ethnic groups who have strong matrilineal or bilateral descents (Cunningham, 2001). Fathers are often the ultimate authority figure within the family, while mothers control the family finances (Abalahin, 1998) and domestic duties at home (Davis et al., 2005). The gender ideology in Indonesia views men as the leaders of the community with decision-making authority while the women are backbones of the family and values (Cunningham, 2001). Hierarchy within the family is important whereby wives are expected to respect their husbands and children should obey their parents and adults older than them (Davis et al., 2005).

Generally, interactions between men and women are monitored closely as premarital sex and dating are not condoned (Abalahin, 1998). Men take responsibility in protecting the women in their family as chastity is highly valued and reflects the family's honor (Abalahin, 1998). The traditional outlet for dating and sexual relationships has been early marriage (Abalahin, 1998).

Marriage marks the milestones where children turn into adults, and it is common for marriages to be viewed as a way of advancing individual and family status in the society (Cunningham, 2001). Marriages between members of different ethnic groups are uncommon except among those who are more educated or live in urban areas (Cunningham, 2001). Collective obligation is also reflected as approval from parents is required when a child seeks to marry (Davis et al., 2005). Social background, education, and characteristics are important considerations when making a spouse selection (Cunningham, 2001). After the marriage, new couples tend to live in the husband's family home or a separate house of their own (Hus & Jarchow, 2008). Divorce occurs very rarely, and the terms vary among various ethnic groups (Cunningham, 2001).

Parenthood is an important milestone to adulthood (Cunningham, 2001), and women in the family including the mother, grandmother, daughters, and sisters often share the responsibility of childcare (Abalahin, 1998). It is very common for parents to coax their children to act favorably in most aspects of their lives (Davis et al., 2005). Children are expected to obey their parents and preserve the family's honor (Davis et al., 2005). In addition, children also depend on their parents until, and sometimes even after, they are married (Abalahin, 1998). Children are also expected to take care of their parents during old age, and older siblings may share the responsibility of taking care of their younger siblings, which may also include paying for their education (Abalahin, 1998). In a group-oriented society that promotes interdependence among each other, disagreements are handled with great care, and personal decisions are strongly conditioned by not bringing shame to the family or groups (Abalahin, 1998). Shame is also often experienced when males or females attract undue attention to themselves or their families (Davis et al., 2005).

Iran

The family unit is seen to be the center for security, warmth, and affection (Hojat & Mehryar, 2003). The extended family is the most common basic social unit in rural areas whereas the nuclear family is a more common unit in urban areas (Jalali, 2005). Regardless which is the most common unit, families maintain a very close psychological bond with their extended families (Jalali, 2005) and bear each other's concerns (Abed-Kotob, 1998c). Nonetheless, with the gradual Western influence that emphasizes nuclear families, some families are beginning to feel conflicted about the extent of their obligations towards their extended families (Jalali, 2005).

In the traditional patriarchal family model, fathers are typically the head of the household (Abed-Kotob, 1998c; Jalali, 2005). They have authority over every member of the family (Jalali, 2005), and they are typically the disciplinarian in the family whose key responsibility is to protect the family's honor (Beeman, 2001). Fathers are also the source of love and affection for the family (Jalali, 2005). When the father dies, the eldest son in the family inherits the authority over the family (Jalali, 2005). On the other hand, mothers also hold an important part in the family with less explicit power and authority (Jalali, 2005). They are typically expected to take care of the domestic chores even if they have professional careers outside the house (Williams, 2008). Although it is gradually changing, a woman typically accepts her husband's dominance (Jalali, 2005) and never openly disagrees with her husband but leverages the help of other family members to intervene on her behalf (Jalali, 2005). Mothers themselves are the mediators should there be a conflict between the father and son (Jalali, 2005). Typically, children live with their parents until they are married, and the family is also responsible for divorced or widowed daughters (Mehryar, Ahmad-Nia, & Jalali-Savar, 2008).

Physical contact between opposite genders is not encouraged, and men and women are not allowed to be alone in the same room with members of the opposite gender who are not their spouse (Beeman, 2001). Premarital sexual relations are strictly not allowed as a girl's virginity is greatly emphasized (Williams, 2008), especially in marriage (Beeman, 2001). Marriage is a socially acceptable way for couples to be united (Hojat & Mehryar, 2003), and it is seen as the most important stage in a person's life (Abed-Kotob, 1998c). It is common for marriages to occur within families through patrilateral parallel cousins or matrilateral cross-cousins as a way to preserve the family heritage and wealth within the families (Beeman, 2001; Hojat & Mehryar, 2003). In marriages that involve someone outside the family, the potential spouse would need visit with the family and discuss the potential union (Beeman, 2001). It is important for families to be agreeable with each other's background because both the families will be bonded together when a couple is married (Beeman, 2001). It also serves as an opportunity for families to extend themselves to different professions and influences (Beeman, 2001) as family connections are important sources of position, security, power, and influence (Jalali, 2005).

Ultimately, parental approval of the potential spouse is the most crucial piece for a marriage to take place (Hojat & Mehryar, 2003). Mothers are normally the primary parent concerned with the children's marriage (Beeman, 2001). They look out for potential spouses for the children (Beeman, 2001) and make the final decision on the spouse (Williams, 2008). Once a potential candidate has been identified, the mother informs her husband of the potential wedding proposal or confers with him to make the formal proposal (Beeman, 2001). It is legally required for women to obtain their father's agreement for marriage (Jalali, 2005). Men are not required by law to obtain approval; however, they still need a moral approval from their father (Jalali, 2005). Children who defy the parental decision are seen as anti-parent, rebellious children (Williams, 2008). However, among the urban upper and middle classes, parental authority is gradually weakening, and young adults are more able to choose their own spouses (Jalali, 2005). This also causes potential conflicts among the young adults as they struggle between a balance of their own independence and their duty to their family (Jalali, 2005).

For the wedding, the groom's family would typically pay for the expenses of the wedding reception (Hojat & Mehryar, 2003) while the bride's family would provide a dowry that consists of household goods and clothing to the couple (Beeman, 2001; Hojat & Mehryar, 2003). Nonetheless, in more modern and educated families, the groom's and bride's families would exchange more non-monetary but spiritually valuable items instead of dowry and payment for ceremony (Hojat & Mehryar, 2003). Polygamy, although legal, is rare (Beeman, 2001; Williams, 2008).

As a method to curb sexual immorality and prostitution, married or single men and unmarried women who are single, divorced, or widowed can also enter into a temporary marriage called 'sigheh' (Hojat & Mehryar, 2003; Williams, 2008). This arrangement requires both parties to agree on the specific duration and compensation payable to the women (Hojat & Mehryar, 2003). Men are able to have multiple wives of such nature at any given time, but women can only be with one man at a time, and each relationship has to have three months or two menstrual cycle periods in between (Hojat & Mehryar, 2003). This occurs more frequently among divorced or widowed women and is highly unpopular among those who are educated (Hojat & Mehryar, 2003).

Divorce is not common as families prefer to stay together despite the circumstances (Beeman, 2001). Often this is also because the families are so entangled with each other that it is difficult to disentangle this close network (Beeman, 2001). However, in cases of divorce, the father becomes the custodian for the son after age two and for the daughter after age seven but remains the provider for his children (Beeman, 2001; Jalali, 2005).

Children are the subjects of familial affection (Jalali, 2005). Mothers are the primary caregivers for children and heavily protect the children's reputation (Beeman, 2001). They learn child-rearing from their own mothers and other female relatives and typically have a very affectionate and devoted relationship with their children, especially the sons (Jalali, 2005). In more wealthy families, servants and nannies may also take an active role in child-rearing (Jalali, 2005). On the other hand, fathers dominate the sons and expect them to take up more responsibilities (Jalali, 2005). Sons are also expected to respect their fathers and take their fathers as role models in preparation for their own future role as the head of the family (Jalali, 2005). Sons are encouraged to be assertive and independent and may still be praised even when they display aggressive behaviors such as bullying their sisters or mothers (Jalali, 2005). Overall, parenting styles are more permissive compared to Western cultures, and children, especially sons, are encouraged to be physically active (Williams, 2008). As a result, boys may grow up with the inclination that they are superior to girls (Jalali, 2005).

Traditionally, older siblings are tasked to take care of their younger siblings (Beeman, 2001). A brother is expected to take care of his sister, and his authority over her is as powerful as a husband's (Jalali, 2005). He is also expected to become her protector should her husband die (Jalali, 2005).

Elderly family members are seen to have more wisdom and normally assume leadership roles in the family (Abed-Kotob, 1998c). Displaying respect for the elderly is very important (Abed-Kotob, 1998c). Children are taught to respect the men in the family and also, by ranking of age, all the adults who are older than them including family and non-family members (Abed-Kotob, 1998c). Aging parents may live in their own residence or with one of their children (Jalali, 2005), and their children bear the full responsibility of taking care of them (Abed-Kotob, 1998c).

Families greatly emphasize education for both genders, and children also are expected to pursue the arts (Beeman, 2001). As the children grow up, older family members are expected to assist them in securing good careers through financial support (Beeman, 2001). Girls who have good internal and external traits are highly treasured as they may attract a marriage that is beneficial for the family (Beeman, 2001).

Iraq

Family loyalty and honor are important values treasured by Iraqis (Attalah, 1998a). Family units are typically close-knit whereby family members are always willing to help each other regardless of whether they live with or near each other (Attalah, 1998a).

The family structure consists of parents, married children and their families, and unmarried children, as well as the paternal grandmother and unmarried aunts (Attalah, 1998a). The paternal grandmother has the most power as her son and daughter-in-law both must obey her (Attalah, 1998a). Nonetheless, the father still has the authority over the household where he makes the final decisions, controls the finances, disciplines, and wields authority over the family (Attalah, 1998a; Pietanza, 2001). On the other hand, the mother dominates and nurtures the home whereby she has control over the children, including adult sons (Attalah, 1998a). Working mothers also are expected to retain all domestic and childcare responsibilities (Pietanza, 2001).

Both genders are taught from a young age to value premarital chastity (Pietanza, 2001). Traditionally, the majority of marriages were arranged with the couple's consent (Attalah, 1998a); however, arranged marriages are becoming rare in modern times (Pietanza, 2001). As marriages signify a union between two families, couples would require each of their parents' approval of the marriage (Pietanza, 2001). Marriage partners typically need to be from the same kin group, although marriage between different ethnic groups is also permitted (Pietanza, 2001). After the wedding, newlywed couples can either live with the husband's family or as a nuclear household (Pietanza, 2001). In an effort by the government to increase the country's population, polygamy marriage became more common as men were encouraged to marry war widows (Pietanza, 2001). Divorce falls under the men's authority, and the custody of the children is granted based on the child's best interest (Pietanza, 2001).

Parents and the family take great responsibility in guiding the next generation as they view it as their duty to groom a good, loyal, and obedient child (Pietanza, 2001). The mother and females from extended families are involved in child-rearing (Pietanza, 2001). Children are well taken care of and disciplined whenever they misbehave (Attalah, 1998a). They are also taught to value and obey elders (Attalah, 1998a; Pietanza, 2001), especially their parents and grandparents (Attalah, 1998a). Boys are precious to the family, and their births are celebrated, whereas girls are viewed as dependents (Pietanza, 2001). Boys are allowed to socialize with older men to learn values and attitudes for the future whereas girls are carefully protected and expected to learn domestic skills (Attalah, 1998a).

JORDAN

Family values play a very important part of the culture in Jordan (Abed-Kotob, 1998d). The family structure contains a large nuclear family and extended families (Schmidt, 2001). The average nuclear family consists of usually five to seven children as women are primarily encouraged to produce children (Abed-Kotob, 1998d). The women's status increases with the number of sons she has (Abed-Kotob, 1998d). The whole family tends to stay in the same home whereby floors are added for married sons and their families (Abed-Kotob, 1998d). Married women are dictated by their husbands (Schmidt, 2001), and daughters-in-law are expected to cook and serve the family (Abed-Kotob, 1998d).

Couples are normally brought together through family introductions (Abed-Kotob, 1998d) or by the father of the bride (Schmidt, 2001). The process of dating and getting to know each other usually begins after the couple has been engaged legally as men and women are typically segregated in public with little interaction between them (Schmidt, 2001). It is common for marriage partners to come from similar backgrounds in terms of lineage, religion, wealth, and education levels (Abed-Kotob, 1998d). Both genders are expected to be single, virtuous, and never married before (Abed-Kotob, 1998d). Women who have had premarital sex and men who frequent night clubs are not favorable candidates for marriage (Abed-Kotob, 1998d). The wedding is a very important event; the expenditure for it is second to a house purchase (Abed-Kotob, 1998d). Due to the cost of weddings, many men from below middle-income families can only wed after they are in their 30s and are able to afford the cost (Abed-Kotob, 1998d). Polygamous marriages are legal (Schmidt, 2001) but rare due to the expensive wedding cost the groom has to afford (Abed-Kotob, 1998d).

Women are encouraged to persevere in their marriage as divorced women are stigmatized by society and rarely remarry (Abed-Kotob, 1998d). After a divorce, the custody of the children automatically goes to the father (Schmidt, 2001).

The birth of a child is joyfully celebrated, and the extended family from the maternal side provides the child's first furniture and wardrobe (Abed-Kotob, 1998d). Women are the primary caregivers to the children (Schmidt, 2001). Typically, girls tend to be more independent (Abed-Kotob, 1998d). This is because parents tend to pamper boys more (Schmidt, 2001). Both parents also adopt the name of their first son after he is born (Schmidt, 2001). Similar to some other Arab countries, education is free and compulsory for both genders (Abed-Kotob, 1998d).

Kuwait

Family units in Kuwait hold the highest priority in a person's life compared to individual, community, or country needs (Abed-Kotob, 1998e). The family structure consists of the parents, married children and their families, and unmarried children, as well as the paternal grandparents

(Abed-Kotob, 1998e). It is preferable for large families to live together in order to maintain familial and cultural traditions (Loew, 2001); however, in urban areas where houses are smaller, extended families tend to live separately but still near to each other (Abed-Kotob, 1998e). Traditionally, men provide a highly protective home environment to the women in the family, and as daughters get married, their husbands continue to take on the protective role (Alsaleh, 2008). Women in religious families are expected to defer all decision-making to the men, and they are limited to socialization within the domestic realm (Alsaleh, 2008). With the increase of modern influences, the role of extended families is gradually giving way to external factors in influencing the younger generation (Alsaleh, 2008). Most of the familial interaction now occurs within the nuclear family rather than the extended family (Alsaleh, 2008).

Socialization between unmarried couples is usually supervised (Alsaleh, 2008). Traditionally, the majority of marriages are arranged within clans (Loew, 2001), between families with long established ties or first cousins (Abed-Kotob, 1998e). Women require their father's consent to marry regardless of age (Loew, 2001). Women must marry a Muslim, but men have the freedom to marry a non-Muslim and legally may marry up to four wives (Loew, 2001). However, in modern times, there are an increasing number of marriages that steer away from these traditional arrangements and are more heterogamous, where they are able to marry those from different nationalities, religions, or ethnicities (Alsaleh, 2008).

Women who have children, especially those who bore sons, gain a higher status in society (Abed-Kotob, 1998e). Education is free (Loew, 2001), and children are provided with outstanding educational opportunities (Alsaleh, 2008). Most schools are segregated by gender after kindergarten (Loew, 2001). Traditionally, women are expected to seek fulfillment through religion, marriage, and parenthood (Alsaleh, 2008); however, intergenerational conflicts are starting to occur between parents and the younger generation as more women are being educated and moving on to roles outside the family (Alsaleh, 2008).

LEBANON

Families are formed on very strong ties (Attalah, 1998b), and they are patriarchal in nature (Darwiche, 2001). The household typically consists of a nuclear family (Darwiche, 2001) with a small size of an average of two children (Attalah, 1998b). As most businesses in the country are owned by families (Attalah, 1998b), the nuclear family tends to maintain close ties with the extended family that also serves as a social security system in challenging times (Darwiche, 2001). Both parents hold equal authority over the children, although mothers typically wield more influence over the children and domestic matters (Darwiche, 2001). Women who have professional careers are still expected to uphold their roles as wives and mothers (Wehbi, 2002). Children typically live with their parents until they are married (Attalah, 1998b).

In terms of marriage, women are more desirable for marriage if their virginity is maintained (Haboush, 2005). Arranged marriages are rare, and due to the economic scene, material factors become key considerations in marriage (Darwiche, 2001). Marriages are also religious affairs as there are no civil marriages (Aprahamian, 2008). Polygamy is rare, although it is legal (Darwiche, 2001).

Children are usually treated with love and affection by their families (Dwairy & Van Sickle, 1996; as cited in Haboush, 2005). Mothers are considered the primary caregivers (Attalah, 1998b). Due to the increase in women in the workforce, it is very common for children to be cared for by babysitters, kindergartens, or extended family members such as grandparents (Darwiche, 2001). Children are raised to depend on their parents for solutions and advice instead of being more independent (Goodnow, Cashmore, Cotton, & Knight, 1984). Children of both genders are also brought up with traditional gender traits whereby brothers would have authority over their sisters while the girls take responsibility to care for their brothers and fathers (Haboush, 2005). In addition, children are also brought up to have deep respects and devotion for their parents (Darwiche, 2001). They take up the responsibility to take care of their parents and grandparents as well as extended family members or neighbors who have no children (Aprahamian, 2008). Typically, boys are highly preferred, and parents' names are given through the son's name, "father of" or "mother of" (Aprahamian, 2008).

Education holds key importance (Darwiche, 2001), and parents view it as a tool to help their children be successful in their future careers (Haboush, 2005). Many parents also prefer to provide moral guidance to their children by sending them to private religious schools (Darwiche, 2001).

Libya

Family life is highly influenced by Islam (Maravilla, 2008) and revolves around tightly knit communities (Abed-Kotob, 1998f). Based on a patriarchal structure, men are the primary breadwinners while the women take care of the home (Maravilla, 2008). The family structure consists of the parents, their unmarried children, and married sons and their nuclear families, as well as extended families including widowed or divorced females (Abed-Kotob, 1998f; Maravilla, 2008). After the death of the father, the son establishes his own household with a similar family structure (Abed-Kotob, 1998f). In modern times, some men establish their own households immediately after marriage instead of living with their parents (Maravilla, 2008). Women are generally encouraged by the government to pursue education and work; hence, working mothers are given incentives, and daycare has been institutionalized by the government since the 1970s (Abed-Kotob, 1998f). Although women were traditionally in charge of domestic duties, there are now more women working outside the household (Jones, 2008).

Adulthood is bestowed upon males after they get married or have children (Maravilla, 2008). Traditionally, men and women are usually not allowed to mix socially in public (Abed-Kotob, 1998f), and premarital romantic relationships are not encouraged (Jones, 2008); hence, most marriages are arranged by the family (Abed-Kotob, 1998f). In modern times, as the social contact between men and women increases, dating is more common, and they tend to meet secretly without the knowledge of their families (Jones, 2008).

Marriage is seen to be a union between families (Jones, 2008), and siblings are married sequentially according to their age (Dalton, 2001). There is a strong tradition that emphasizes the patrilineal descent whereby men are supposed to marry their paternal uncle's daughter (Dalton, 2001; Jones, 2008). Known as the 'first right,' the male cousin needs to waive his rights to marry before the woman can marry another (Dalton, 2001; Jones, 2008). Nonetheless, those who marry by love must seek their families' approval (Abed-Kotob, 1998f), and the women must provide their consent for the marriage to be lawful (Jones, 2008; Maravilla, 2008). Although the older generation traditionally prefers marriages to be within the extended family (Dalton, 2001; Jones, 2008), some families may also use marriages to bond with another family for other mutual benefits (Dalton, 2001). Women have equal status as men under the law (Jones, 2008), and they may file a petition with the court to be allowed to marry in the event their father opposes it (Jones, 2008; Maravilla, 2008). In addition, women are expected to be virgins when they marry (Jones, 2008), and the more highly esteemed (Jones, 2008) or distantly related (Dalton, 2001) the bride is, the higher the amount money involved (Jones, 2008; Maravilla, 2008). A non-Muslim man is expected to become a Muslim if he marries a Muslim woman; however, if a Muslim man marries a non-Muslim woman, she does not need to convert, but their children must be brought up as Muslims (Jones, 2008). Polygamy is allowed in Libya, but the husbands would need their first wife's consent before they are able to marry another wife (Jones, 2008).

In Libyan families, fathers are usually eager to have a male heir in the family, and they are generally very fond of children and often pamper them (Jones, 2008). Children are taught and expected to be respectful to elders and courteous to others even in public (Abed-Kotob, 1998f). It is common for children to take care of their elderly family members as they are never sent to retirement or old-age homes (Abed-Kotob, 1998f).

Malaysia

Family and marriage play an important role in an individual's life whereby the family matters and interests take precedence over wealth and material goods (Bala, 1998; King, 2008). The family structure consists of the parents and children (King, 2008), and the predominant arrangement remains the parents with an unmarried child (Kukreja, 2003). Although nuclear families are gradually becoming more common, family members still keep a close connection and depend on each other for support (Bala, 1998; King, 2008). The family unit is often defined by hierarchy whereby the oldest male leads the family and relations are ranked by age and seniority (King, 2008). With migration to urban areas and the dispersion of family members, it is common during major festive holidays for married couples and their families to return to their parents' houses or their hometowns to unite with other extended family members (Williamson, 2001). This also provides an opportunity for siblings and cousins from extended families to establish friendly companionship as they are the preferred source of playmates (Williamson, 2001).

Generally, couples are not encouraged to live together before getting married (King, 2008), and it is considered inappropriate for dating as well as married couples to publicly display affection for each other (Bala, 1998). Non-Muslims who marry Muslims, regardless of gender, are expected to convert to become Muslims (Williamson, 2001). Therefore, the union has to be registered with the religious authority in addition to the government registration (Williamson, 2001). On the other hand, non-Muslim couples from different ethnic backgrounds who wish to marry are only answerable to their own families and beliefs, which may often pose considerable stress as well (Williamson, 2001).

The meeting between prospective in-laws is considered a crucial process to ensure marriage success as marriage is believed to be the union of the two families as well (Williamson, 2001). Newlywed couples who have yet to establish their households may live with their parents for a specific period of time before moving out on their own (King, 2008). Wives are expected to be respectful and defer to their husbands (Bala, 1998). Both husband and wife play an equal role in taking care of their children (Bala, 1998).

Parents take great pride in their children (King, 2008), and they are lavished with great care (Williamson, 2001). Extended families, including the grandmother of the newborn, often live together with them during the first few months (Williamson, 2001). As it is common for both men and women to be in the workforce, domestic servants, often foreign women, are hired to assist with domestic duties as well as childcare (Bala, 1998; King, 2008; See, 2008). Nonetheless, family members are still the preferred source for childcare (King, 2008).

In addition, parents devout time and resources to ensure that their children, regardless of gender, receive a good education in order to have a good start and be successful in life (King, 2008). Children from more affluent families are often sent to overseas universities to pursue a better education (Williamson, 2001). Children are also expected to take care of their parents (Bala, 1998), and there are some aging or widowed parents who live with their married children and help with household tasks such as childcare (King, 2008). Children are also expected to be respectful to all adults older than them (King, 2008). They are taught to use proper titles when addressing adults as part of the observation of age hierarchy (Williamson, 2001). Older siblings are also expected to be responsible for taking care of their younger siblings, which may include paying for their education and assisting them in their careers (King, 2008). In some families, the children are also expected to assist in the family business as part of their social obligation to their family (King, 2008). Every member in the family is expected to behave decently to avoid criticism as identity, honor, and the judgment of others hold great importance to them and their families (King, 2008).

Morocco

The needs and desires of one's extended family are understood to be of upmost importance for Moroccans (Bechtold, 2008). It is understood that one's reputation is reflected upon all members of his or her extended family (Johnston, 2001). Roles in the family are gender specific, although strict adherences to these gender roles are beginning to relax (York, 2009). The father is the head of the household, but both men and women play an important role in decision-making (Abed-Kotob, 1998g). Girls are expected to help their mothers with household tasks to prepare for an adult life in the domestic sphere while boys, on the other hand, are expected to spend time outside, to prepare for a future in the public sphere (Bechtold, 2008). A typical household in Morocco is comprised of a man's wife, children, parents, and unmarried siblings (York, 2009). The elderly enjoy a high level of respect and expect to be taken care of by family members when they become old (Abed-Kotob, 1998g). Moroccans rarely, if ever, live alone. If students must move away from their parents for college, they tend to live with extended family members near the university.

All Moroccans are expected to get married (Abed-Kotob, 1998g). Marriages are not typically arranged, but parents have a say in who their children marry, for the status of one's prospective partner reflects greatly upon the family. In 2004, the minimum age for marriage increased from 15 to 18 and permission from a woman's male guardian was no longer legally required for marriage (Bechtold, 2008). Divorce is allowed in Morocco but looked down upon (Abed-Kotob, 1998g). In the past, the decision to divorce was made solely by the husband, but today, both partners have a legal say in the matter. Divorce typically results in lowered status for women, and it is very difficult for a woman to provide for herself or remarry after a divorce (Johnston, 2001).

Practically all Moroccan women aspire to be mothers (Abed-Kotob, 1998g). Girls and boys are socialized separately at home, but they interact more at school (Bechtold, 2008). Daughters are expected to help their mothers with household chores while sons are not expected to do so. Education is highly valued but isn't always the first priority for children whose families don't have much money (York, 2009). Especially among families of lower socioeconomic status, girls are taken out of school at a young age in order to help their mothers take care of the home (Johnston, 2001). Public education is free through university (Abed-Kotob, 1998g). The children of wealthy Moroccans are often educated abroad (Johnston, 2001).

Oman

In Oman, family and tribal ties hold great importance (Abed-Kotob, 1998h). Husbands hold the greatest authority within their households, but their wives have considerable say concerning family and household matters (Chatty & Peterson, 2001). The traditional domestic unit in Oman includes the male head of the household, his wives, his sons, and his sons' wives and their children. Members of this multigenerational family often live together in the same home or keep in very close contact with each other. The oldest male of a household is responsible for all of the family members and their property (Daadaoui, 2008) while the eldest female is in charge of delegating household tasks (Chatty & Peterson, 2001). Gender roles in the family are traditional. Men are expected to be the family's breadwinners while women are expected to stay at home to run the household (Abed-Kotob, 1998h). A woman's conduct in society is understood to reflect greatly upon her family, and any misconduct could potentially destroy her family's reputation (Daadaoui, 2008).

Most marriages in Oman are arranged and are viewed as contracts between families as opposed to contracts between husbands and wives (Chatty & Peterson, 2001). Omanis tend to marry within their particular ethnic group (Daadaoui, 2008). Preference is made for marriages between cousins (Abed-Kotob, 1998h). The minimum age required for marriage is 18 years (Daadaoui, 2008). In Omani, a dowry is gifted to the bride as opposed to the bride's family (Abed-Kotob, 1998h). Before the wedding, the bride receives a portion of the dowry to spend on herself and her home. The second portion of the dowry is an agreed-upon amount that the husband will pay his wife in case of divorce. Divorce may only be initiated by the husband (Daadaoui, 2008) and is relatively rare (Abed-Kotob, 1998h). After divorce, women return to live with their parents.

Newborns distract very little from the regular family routine. Infants grow up alongside their mothers and are expected to watch more than interact (Chatty & Peterson, 2001). After the age of two, children are encouraged to act like adults and take on roles in the house such as hospitality towards guests very early in life. Omani citizens as well as their government place high value on education (Daadaoui, 2008). Approximately 10% of the state budget goes towards education, the majority of schools are publicly funded, and the government has invested in educational reforms. Although school attendance is not compulsory, attendance rates are high and relatively equal between boys and girls.

Pakistan

The family plays a central role in Pakistani society (Nath, 2005). Collective family identity comes before individual identity. Households in Pakistan are often multigenerational (Lodrick, 1998b). It is typical that a new bride will move into her husband's family home. Women are typically homemakers while men are responsible for being breadwinners (Howard, 2001). Families in Pakistan are patrilineal and hierarchical (Nath, 2005). The oldest male is the head of the household and has the greatest say in family matters, but women's opinions are also considered (Lodrick, 1998b). Nursing homes do not exist in Pakistan (Nath, 2005). If the family cannot afford to hire a nurse, it is the responsibility of the female family members to care for their elderly relatives.

Marriages are typically arranged (Lodrick, 1998b) and are understood to be not simply a union between a couple, but as a union of families (Howard, 2001). The length of an engagement depends upon the ages of the bride and groom and may last from a few months to a few years (Nath, 2005). In some cases, couples first meet on the day of their wedding. Weddings are elaborate and are celebrated separately by men and women. Pakistanis tend to marry within their caste to a greater extent in agricultural communities and to a lesser extent in urban areas (Lodrick, 1998b). Castes in Pakistan are defined by profession and income and do not reflect the religious dimensions of a Hindu caste. In Islam, a man is allowed to have up to four wives if he can care for them all equally (Nath, 2005). Polygamy is not typical, yet it is still practiced in Pakistan.

Children are considered to be blessings (Howard, 2001). A woman's status increases in the eyes of her husband and family when she gives birth to a son (Lodrick, 1998b). Nuclear families in Pakistan are typically large (Nath, 2005). According to a 1997 study, the average Pakistani woman bears seven children in her lifetime. In Pakistan, various ceremonies take place as rites of passage in infancy (Howard, 2001). Male infants are circumcised and their heads are shaved (Lodrick, 1998b). Traditionally, the grandfather names a newborn within 40 days of birth (Howard, 2001). It is also tradition that a baby's first garment is sewn from the grandfather's old shirt. Since its independence, Pakistan has expanded its educational facilities. Despite this effort, school attendance and literacy rates are low especially in rural areas, where children must work in the fields to help support their families (Lodrick, 1998b).

Saudi Arabia

Family networks play a fundamental role in Saudi society and culture, and cross-generational ties are emphasized (DeLong-Bas, 2008). Traditionally, an individual's status was based primarily upon the reputation of one's family of origin, but today, an individual's merits and achievements are beginning to play a larger role. Proper demeanor and conduct, especially of women, play a critical role in the maintenance of the family's honor.

Extended family members often live together in the same household (Abed-Kotob, 1998i). Children are expected to live with their parents until they are married, and after marriage, wives often move into their husband's family home (DeLong-Bas, 2008). Today, young couples are beginning to break this tradition. Many must move away from their family homes due to the location of jobs and universities. Lifetime responsibility to one's extended family, especially to siblings and parents, is emphasized in Saudi culture. Older siblings care for younger siblings, and brothers are responsible for protecting their sisters. Decisions that affect the family are often made by group consensus. Men may have a greater say in family decision-making, but women and children play an active role. Elderly family members are also looked towards in the family decision-making process, and their input is highly regarded. Women are fairly restricted in Saudi society and may not mingle with men who are not close family members (Abed-Kotob, 1998i). It is up to the men of the household to protect their female family members from outside contact (DeLong-Bas,

2008). Although some Saudi women work outside the home, it is believed that a woman's first priority should be to her duties within the home.

In Saudi Arabia, it is required for a groom to pay his bride a dowry before a couple is to be legally married (Abed-Kotob, 1998i). This law makes it difficult for some young men to afford marriage. A bride's consent is required for marriage, but the marriage is primarily arranged by her family, and the contract itself is handled by her father or guardian (DeLong-Bas, 2008). Saudi women do not change their last name when they are married because they legally belong to their families of origin even after a marriage occurs (Abed-Kotob, 1998i). In urban areas, young couples are rejecting the traditional arrangement of marriages and are looking increasingly for greater compatibility, emotional fulfillment, and shared interest with their partners (DeLong-Bas, 2008).

Divorce may be initiated by both men and women and is fairly common in Saudi Arabia (Abed-Kotob, 1998i). Today, more divorces are occurring due to issues of compatibility especially among those who are highly educated and have studied abroad (DeLong-Bas, 2008). In the case of divorce or death of a spouse, it is expected that both men and women return to live with their parents. Custody of young children is given to the mother. After boys reach the age of five and girls reach the age of seven, custody is handed over to the father. This automatic assignment of custody has been challenged in recent years, and courts are beginning to award custody of older children to the mothers if living conditions in the father's home are deemed unsuitable. Remarriage is common, especially among men (Cole, 2001).

Both marriage and childbearing are expected norms in Saudi culture (DeLong-Bas, 2008). Motherhood is revered, and the birth of a child, especially that of a son, is occasion for celebration. Mothers and other women in the household take on most of the responsibility for childcare with the exception that fathers are looked towards to prepare their older sons for adulthood. Today, it is becoming more common for foreign domestic servants and maids to take on the primary duties of childcare (Cole, 2001). Children are socialized by all members of their family to be polite, hospitable, and obedient (DeLong-Bas, 2008). Boys are raised to become the family's providers and protectors while girls are socialized to be nurturing and to take care of the household (Abed-Kotob, 1998i). Education is a central part of Saudi culture, and parents are very involved in their children's education. Preschool through to university education is state funded and free to all citizens. Male and female students are educated separately. Practically all children attend school through age 12, but many do not continue their education beyond that point. Today, at least half of all university graduates are women (Cole, 2001).

SOMALIA

Family structure in Somalia is clan based and follows the male line (Glascock, 1998). Somali households are typically composed of extended family members (Affi, 2003). Women are held primarily responsible for childcare and housework (Surgin, 2001). In farming clans, men typically take care of camels and cattle, women are in charge of planting and harvesting, and children tend to the goats and sheep. In urban areas, both men and women may work outside the home. Traditionally, Somali women are expected to submit to their husbands and play a supporting role in the family, but because so many husbands were lost in the civil war, many Somali women have taken on many traditional male roles and have become their family's household heads and breadwinners (Affi, 2003).

Marriages in Somalia are considered to be not only a union between two people, but, more importantly, a union or alliance between two families (Surgin, 2001). Marriages are typically arranged, although lately, there has been more room for individual choice. It is common for newlyweds to move into the husband's family home after marriage. Men usually wait to marry until they have accumulated some property and cattle (Glascock, 1998). New brides are usually much younger than their husbands. Polygamy is legal, but not common. On the other hand, divorce is very common. If a divorce occurs, women usually keep custody of their children (Surgin, 2001). Due to the high rate of divorce, many children grow up in single-parent households.

It is a goal of Somali parents to have many children (Glascock, 1998). Children can assist their parents around the house and farm and are expected to care for their parents in old age (Surgin, 2001). Because Somali households typically include extended family members, mothers receive plenty of assistance with childcare duties (Affi, 2003).

The civil war of the 1990s took a large toll on Somalia's educational system (Glascock, 1998). Since the war, private schools emerged in the absence of a nationally run school system (Affi, 2003). Quranic schooling, featuring a curriculum based upon memorization of the Quran, is the primary educational system available in rural areas (Glascock, 1998). In urban areas, some technical schools, secular private schools, and universities either survived the war or have reemerged alongside the Quranic schools (Affi, 2003). Local public school systems are developing in more peaceful parts of the country. Somali boys have greater opportunities for education than Somali girls. Quranic schools usually may only be attended by boys (Glascock, 1998), and because many Somali mothers now work outside the home, daughters are not able to attend school because they must take over housework and childcare duties (Affi, 2003).

SUDAN

The family is at the center of Sudanese life (Kenyon, 1998). Typically, extended family members either live together in the same household or near one another (Stanford, 2001b). Newlyweds will move into the wife's family home for about a year or until their first child is born. At that point, they will move into a home close in proximity to the wife's family home. As young people move into cities, nuclear households are becoming more common (Halim, 2003). Even when young Sudanese must move away from their families, they make a point to stay in close contact. Kinship connections are maintained through both their father's and mother's sides (Stanford, 2001b), but greater significance is placed upon ties through the father's side (El-Hassan, 2008). Sudanese society is patriarchal, and women hold a lesser status than men (Kenyon, 1998). Women are in charge of all childcare and household duties (Stanford, 2001b). Women are increasingly starting to work outside the home but are restricted to jobs deemed suitable for women (Kenyon, 1998). Men and women typically socialize with members of their same sex (Stanford, 2001b). Men socialize with one another in public settings while women meet at home.

Marriages are typically arranged by the family even among educated and wealthy Sudanese. The preferred marriage is between cousins, and it is important that marriages stay between members of the same tribe and social class. Usually marriage arrangements do not involve any input from the couple, and it is not uncommon for a bride and groom to meet for the first time on their wedding day. Grooms are typically much older than their brides because they need to be able to financially support a family before they are married as well as pay a bride-price (Stanford, 2001b). Polygamy is legal and understood as a way of extending family relations and support

(El-Hassan, 2008). Divorce is considered shameful and understood as breaking family support ties. Despite this perspective, divorce rates in Sudan are rising (Stanford, 2001b). The process of divorce is more difficult for women than for men (Halim, 2003). Men may initiate divorce without court proceedings, but women who seek a divorce must go through a court of law. Mothers are automatically given custody of sons up to age seven and daughters up to age nine. At that point, custody then shifts to the father.

Large families are desired in Sudan (Kenyon, 1998). The family prefers the birth of sons over daughters. Mothers are responsible for the children's physical well-being while fathers are responsible for their guidance (Halim, 2003). Girls and boys are raised and educated separately until high school. School attendance in Sudan is not compulsory (El-Hassan, 2008). Girls typically spend less time enrolled in school than boys because parents view it to be more useful for girls to spend time learning domestic skills at home (Stanford, 2001b). Sudan has a tradition of Quranic schooling, or a curriculum focused on memorizing the Qur'an (Kenyon, 1998). More recently, secular education is being incorporated alongside religious education.

Syria

Family structures and norms vary greatly between rural and urban areas (Abi-Hashem, 2003). Syrians identify strongly with members of their immediate and extended families (Stanford, 2001c) and often live with members of their extended family (Stanford, 2001c). Due to a housing shortage, household composition in urban areas is often determined by necessity rather than choice (Abi-Hashem, 2003). In some cases, dwellings must be shared with people who are not relatives. It is expected that children continue to live with their parents until they are married (Standish, 2010) and that parents will in turn be cared for by their children in old age (Stanford, 2001c). Women and men are granted equal rights under the constitution, but social norms and expectations of women prevent them from regularly exercising their rights (Abed-Kotob, 1998j). Women in Syria are legally allowed to work outside the home, although it is still relatively rare (Stanford, 2001c). As time goes on, more and more women are starting to enter the workforce (Abi-Hashem, 2003).

Traditionally marriages are arranged by families (Stanford, 2001c). Although there is more space now for individual choice in a marriage partner, young couples rarely marry against their parents' wishes. The marriage rate is declining in Syria due to inflation, housing shortages, and inability to pay for the cost of the wedding and the dowry. Young women are encouraged to wait to marry until they receive a proposal from someone who has a certain level of financial security (Standish, 2010). Polygamy is legal but not commonly practiced (Abi-Hashem, 2003). The Islamic understanding that a man may only take additional wives if he can care for each of them equally is legally enforced in Syria (Stanford, 2001c). A judge may refuse to approve of a polygamous marriage if a man does not supply evidence that he is financially capable of supporting more than one wife (Abi-Hashem, 2003).

Motherhood is a revered role for Syrian women, and raising children is understood to be a woman's primary duty (Standish, 2010). Children are understood to be blessings (Stanford, 2001c). Parents with many children are considered fortunate because they can assist with field and housework, and a greater number of children provide parents with greater assurance that they will be cared for in old age. Despite this point of view, the average number of children in families has fallen from 8 to 10 down to 3 in recent years (Stanford, 2001c). Parents with high levels of education typically have fewer children (Abi-Hashem, 2003). This may be due to a trend among the educated to delay marriage, resulting in reduced reproductive years (Abi-Hashem, 2008). Although at times children are punished harshly, parents are typically very affectionate towards their children (Stanford, 2001c). Mothers have an especially close bond with their sons.

School in Syria is compulsory from age 8 to 14 and free through university (Abi-Hashem, 2008). Boys and girls are educated separately after age 13 (Stanford, 2001c). In recent years, major improvements have been made throughout the country's education system, but there is still much room for improvement. There is a gap between the quality of education available in rural and urban schools (Abi-Hashem, 2008).

TUNISIA

Family is at the center of life in Tunisia. Traditionally, multigenerational families lived together and shared resources and household duties. Although this is still sometimes the case, most households are now comprised solely of the nuclear family (Issitt, 2008b). Despite this shift,

Tunisians still maintain strong kinship ties. Tunisians rarely live alone (Zarr, 2009). Young adults usually do not move out of their parents' homes until they get married. In Tunisian families, the male is the head of the household. Traditionally, men worked outside the home while women were left in charge of household duties (Issit, 2008). With help from government initiatives to encourage female education, careers, marriage rights, and family planning, many women in Tunisia work outside the home, and about 50% of college graduates are women (Zarr, 2009). Today, men and women have equal legal rights concerning inheritance, property ownership, child custody, and divorce (Abed-Kotob, 1998k). Despite this shift towards an egalitarian social structure, gender equality is still far from a reality in Tunisia. Even with careers outside the home, women are still understood to be solely responsible for household duties, and as they enter the public sphere, they face a very male-dominated society (Hopkins, 2001).

In some cases, marriages are arranged by families, but the decision to marry is becoming increasingly up to individuals (Hopkins, 2001). A young couple will almost always ask for their parents' consent if they are interested in marriage (Zarr, 2009). Tunisians have an awareness of economic class, and women are not supposed to marry a man who is of a lower status (Issit, 2008b). Polygamous and forced marriages are illegal, and the minimum age for marriage is 20 for men and 17 for women (Abed-Kotob, 1998k).

In Tunisia, children are understood to be blessings (Zarr, 2009). Newborns are typically cared for by their mothers, but beyond this initial life stage, fathers assist in child-rearing, playing a greater role in the upbringing of their sons than their daughters (Hopkins, 2001). Older siblings and extended family members will assist with childcare duties (Zarr, 2009). Public education is free through university (Abed-Kotob, 1998k) and is compulsory through the age of 16 (Zarr, 2009). Male and female children take classes together. Schools are modeled after the French system (Abed-Kotob, 1998k), and children are taught in French and Arabic as well as English (Issit, 2008b). After primary school, children may stay in the regular school system or attend trade school.

Turkey

The family is a very strong social institution in Turkey (Gursoy, 2003). The typical household is nuclear, yet one's extended family members usually live nearby. Family members in Turkey are very committed to one another. Individuals can expect support from their family in times of crisis or need. Turks have great respect for elders, and it is assumed that children will care for their parents in old age. One's individual status is defined by his or her family's image. It is very important that an individual act in a way that will not embarrass or shame his or her family. Although there are a growing number of female working professionals, women typically play a subservient role in the family (Tyson, 1998). In the eyes of the government, women and men have equal legal rights, but traditionally, the household is male dominated (Magnarella, 2001).

The great majority of adults in Turkey are married, and divorce is very uncommon. When divorce does occur, both men and women tend to remarry (Magnarella, 2001). Individuals almost always marry within their own ethnic groups and religious sects. In 1926, secular law replaced sharia law. Today, the Turkish government only recognizes civil marriage ceremonies (Gursoy, 2003). Polygamous marriages are not allowed, and the consent of both the bride and groom are required to marry (Magnarella, 2001). Although the vast majority of marriages in Turkey are consensual, the family typically screens and recommends potential spouses for their children (Magnarella, 2001). Especially in rural areas, women still marry at young ages, and parents work out a financial agreement between the two joining families (Tyson, 1998).

Children are highly valued in Turkey and are desired by practically all married couples (Gursoy, 2003). Traditionally, sons are preferred over daughters. Giving birth to a son will increase the status of a woman in the eyes of her husband, extended family, and community (Magnarella, 2001). Boys are circumcised after the age of seven as a rite of passage into adulthood (Tyson, 1998). In Turkey, the father is understood to be the authority figure, and his relationship with his children, especially his daughters, is typically more formal. Mothers in Turkey are usually warm, nurturing, and protective of their children (Magnarella, 2001). Girls are socialized to be helpful, modest, obedient, and virtuous while boys are expected to be brave, proud, and assertive. Children are taught a strict code of respect. Harsh and physical punishments are common (Gursoy, 2003). School is required for children until they reach age 14 (Magnarella, 2001). School attendance is encouraged beyond that point, but it is not always a reality (Tyson, 1998). Quality of educational facilities varies throughout the country and is typically worse in rural areas. Many rural areas do not have high schools, making it very difficult for the children who reside in these communities to continue their education.

United Arab Emirates

Life in the United Arab Emirates (UAE) centers around the family (Abed-Kotob, 1998b). The tribal or kin group plays an important role in shaping one's social standing and identity (Khalaf, 2001). Although most households are comprised of the nuclear family, extended family members often live close by. Women have primary authority in the domestic sphere. They are considered responsible for household duties and parenting but often receive assistance from live-in domestic servants. Men and women have equal legal rights, but society is primarily patriarchal. Men and women stay relatively separate when out in public. This separation limits women's potential career paths. Women find work in the fields of education, civil service, and health while politics and religion only employ men.

Most marriages in UAE are arranged and occur between members of the same tribe (Khalaf, 2001). Although this is still a prevailing pattern, today there is more space for individual choice in one's marriage partner. A formal contract negotiated between families is involved in all marriages (Wright, 2003). Some topics covered in the marriage contract include permission for a woman to work, continue her education, or regularly visit her parents. The practice of polygamy is not common in UAE, but men are allowed up to four wives if they can care for each equally (Khalaf, 2001).

Marriage is a primary goal for Emirian women (Wright, 2003). Girls are understood to become women when they are married (Briegel, 2008). Unless one's husband is very strict, a woman is usually allowed more freedom after marriage. If a divorce occurs, a woman usually returns to live with her parents. Upon this return, her parents may be strict with her and treat her like a 'girl' again.

Weddings in UAE are often very large and usually only attended by women (Wright, 2003). Men receive a monetary incentive from the government for marrying a UAE national (Khalaf, 2001). Both men and women in the United Arab Emirates are legally allowed to initiate divorce, but the process is more difficult for women (Wright, 2003).

Large families are common and encouraged in the UAE (Wright, 2003). There is no strong parental preference for boys over girls; all children are understood to be blessings. Although mothers are the primary caregivers (Wright, 2003), fathers, relatives, and foreign servants all play a role in raising children (Khalaf, 2001). Parents in UAE are very affectionate towards their children. Children are taught to be very respectful to their parents and elders. From an early age, girls are given more responsibility in the household and boys are allowed more freedom (Briegel, 2008).

Children are further socialized through the school system (Khalaf, 2001). Boys and girls are educated separately, but each gender follows the same curriculum (Briegel, 2008). In UAE the literacy rates for women are higher than those for men. University education is highly valued. School is free through university level, and the government offers full scholarships for study-abroad programs (Abed-Kotob, 1998b). In conjunction with its public school system, UAE has a well-established private education system (Briegel, 2008). UAE's rate of university attendance is the highest in the world (Khalaf, 2001). More women than men attend universities, but fewer of these women go on to use their education in the workforce.

Yemen

Households in Yemen may be comprised of the nuclear family, patrilineal extended family members, or shared by the families of two brothers (Rodionov, 2001). Yemeni people almost never live alone (Dahlgren, 2003). Divorced, widowed, or unmarried individuals are welcomed into the homes of their extended family members. Yemeni people closely associate with a tribe or kin group that follows the male line (Rodionov, 2001). Typically, men are the family's financial providers and act as the head of the household. Women's responsibilities include taking care of the children and the home. Women and men have relatively equal legal rights, but socially and culturally, Yemen is still very male dominated. Religious authorities recommend gender segregation, limiting the potential options for women to work outside the home. Strictness of gender segregation varies regionally as well as between rural and urban areas (Dahlgren, 2003).

Both men and women aspire to be married. Marriages are typically arranged by families. A young man's female relatives will suggest potential brides, and his father will be responsible for the final choice in marriage partner (Rodionov, 2001). Before the bride-to-be's father prepares the marriage contract, he usually considers her opinion in the matter. Polygamy is legal in Yemen, but uncommon. Traditionally, a preferred marriage would be between first cousins. Divorce is a relatively simple process in Yemen (Daeg de Mott, 1998b). There is little social stigma attached to it. Divorce occurs more frequently in Yemen than it does in neighboring countries.

Women typically marry at a young age and start having children early on in a marriage (Daeg de Mott, 1998b). Children are highly valued, and families are typically large. Most families have a preference for boys (Dahlgren, 2003). It is understood to be important for women to give birth to at least one boy to continue the family lineage. Young children are typically cared for by their mothers and older sisters (Rodionov, 2001). Mothers are often indulgent, and children typically are not punished. Under the age of four, children are understood as not capable of self-control.

In the past, formal education was only accessible to children of wealthy families (Daeg de Mott, 1998b). Today, the Yemeni government provides free public education (Rodionov, 2001). Due to high population growth, there are more school-aged children than there are classrooms and teachers (Dahlgren, 2003). Especially when classroom space is in high demand, families place a higher priority on their sons' education than their daughters'. Due to varying resources, histories, and social norms, female access to education varies greatly among different regions in Yemen. Girls and boys are educated separately from primary school through higher education (Rodionov, 2001). Today, some women attend college, but admission priority is still given to men (Daeg de Mott, 1998b).

Clinical Implications

Many Muslims ask: "Why are you focusing on Muslim families as a different group? We are just human beings like everyone else." While it is true that in many ways Muslim families are just like other people, in some other ways Muslim families are unique. There are universal or core similarities shared by all humans, but there are also cultural differences among groups of people. As we can see from reviewing the cultural and family characteristics of the aforementioned countries, it is apparent that it is quite challenging to describe the relationship between Muslim men and women and their relational and familial approaches to life events without considering the differences. Every society has its own set of local, ethnic, social, and historical factors that impact the interpretation and application of the Islamic faith. These different cultural and contextual issues will determine the interpretation of Islam in terms of how traditional or flexible and open Islam can be. Most importantly, family members' attitudes and an individual's own sense of identity in relation to his or her cultural background influence every Muslim family differently. This is sometimes to the point that even family members have difficulty separating cultural issues from Islamic perspectives. Furthermore, in many Western countries, there has often been confusion regarding what characteristics come from being raised as a Muslim.

It is important to note that religious ideology and cultural belief systems strongly influence the way family problems are understood and dealt with. It is also important to note that the collectivist culture of Muslim families strongly encourages placing high value on the family and individual integration process and not much value on the differentiation process. Furthermore, considering rudimentary ideas about gender relationships, family life, marriage, and divorce based on Islamic ideology helps clinicians understand family members' life dilemmas more comprehensively. The goal is to respect Muslim families' sense of religious identity and interactional patterns while challenging their dysfunctional family dynamics.

REFERENCES

Abalahin, A.J. (1998). Indonesians. In T. Gall (Ed.), *Encyclopedia of cultures and daily life: Asia and Oceania* (Vol. 3, pp. 301–302). Detroit: Gale.

Abed-Kotob, S. (1998a). Algeria. In T. Gall (Ed.), *Encyclopedia of cultures and daily life: Africa* (Vol. 1, pp. 20–21). Detroit: Gale.

Abed-Kotob, S. (1998b). Emirians. In T. Gall (Ed.), *Encyclopedia of cultures and daily life: Asia and Oceania* (Vol. 3, pp. 194–195). New York: Worldmark.

Abed-Kotob, S. (1998c). Iranians. In T. Gall (Ed.), *Encyclopedia of cultures and daily life: Asia and Oceania* (Vol. 3, pp. 308–309). Detroit: Gale.

Abed-Kotob, S. (1998d). Jordanians. In T. Gall (Ed.), *Encyclopedia of cultures and daily life: Asia and Oceania* (Vol. 3, pp. 351–353). Detroit: Gale.

Abed-Kotob, S. (1998e). Kuwaitis. In T. Gall (Ed.), *Encyclopedia of cultures and daily life: Asia and Oceania* (Vol. 3, pp. 420–421). Detroit: Gale.

Abed-Kotob, S. (1998f). Libyans. In T. Gall (Ed.), *Encyclopedia of cultures and daily life: Africa* (Vol. 1, pp. 256–257). Detroit: Gale.

Abed-Kotob, S. (1998g). Moroccans. In T. Gall (Ed.), *Encyclopedia of cultures and daily life: Africa* (Vol. 1, pp. 303–304). New York: Worldmark.

Abed-Kotob, S. (1998h). Omanis. In T. Gall (Ed.), *Encyclopedia of cultures and daily life: Asia and Oceania* (Vol. 3, p. 597). New York: Worldmark.

Abed-Kotob, S. (1998i). Saudis. In T. Gall (Ed.), *Encyclopedia of cultures and daily life: Asia and Oceania* (Vol. 3, p. 679). New York: Worldmark.

Abed-Kotob, S. (1998j). Syrians. In T. Gall (Ed.), *Encyclopedia of cultures and daily life: Asia and Oceania* (Vol. 3, pp. 726–727). New York: Worldmark.

Abed-Kotob, S. (1998k). Tunisians. In T. Gall (Ed.), *Encyclopedia of cultures and daily life: Asia and Oceania* (Vol. 3, pp. 440–442). New York: Worldmark.

Abi-Hashem, N. (2003). Syria. In B. Sherif-Trask & L. Walter (Eds.), *The Greenwood encyclopedia of women's issues worldwide: North Africa and the Middle East* (Vol. 4, pp. 260–267). Westport, CT: Greenwood Press.

Abi-Hashem, N. (2008). Syria. In I. Epstein & G. Talhami (Eds.), *The Greenwood encyclopedia of children's issues worldwide: North Africa and the Middle East* (Vol. 4, pp. 274–282). Westport, CT: Greenwood Press.

Affi, L. (2003). Somalia. In A. Tripp & L. Walter (Eds.), *The Greenwood encyclopedia of women's issues worldwide: Sub-Saharan Africa* (Vol. 6, pp. 391–395). Westport, CT: Greenwood Press.

Alsaleh, A. (2008). Kuwait. In I. Epstein & G.H. Talhami (Eds.), *The Greenwood encyclopedia of children's issues worldwide: North Africa and the Middle East* (pp. 113–114). Westport, CT: Greenwood Press.

Aprahamian, S. (2008). Lebanon. In I. Epstein & G.H. Talhami (Eds.), *The Greenwood encyclopedia of children's issues worldwide: North Africa and the Middle East* (pp. 128–129). Westport, CT: Greenwood Press.

Assaad, R., Levision, D., & Zibani, N. (2005). *The effect of child work on schooling: evidence from Egypt.* Working Paper No. 2005–10, University of Minnesota, Minnesota, Minnesota Population Center. As cited in Rowe, M., & Rizzo, H. (2008). Egypt. In I. Epstein & G.H. Talhami (Eds.), *The Greenwood encyclopedia of children's issues worldwide: North Africa and the Middle East* (pp. 48–51). Westport, CT: Greenwood Press.

Attalah, H. (1998a). Iraqis. In T. Gall (Ed.), *Encyclopedia of cultures and daily life: Asia and Oceania* (Vol. 3, pp. 315–316). Detroit: Gale.

Attalah, H. (1998b). Lebanese. In T. Gall (Ed.), *Encyclopedia of cultures and daily life: Asia and Oceania* (Vol. 3, pp. 435–436). Detroit: Gale.

Bala, P. (1998). Malaysian Malays. In T. Gall (Ed.), *Encyclopedia of cultures and daily life: Asia and Oceania* (Vol. 3, pp. 470–473). Detroit: Gale.

Bechtold, B.H. (2008). Morocco. In I. Epstein & G. Talhami (Eds.), *The Greenwood encyclopedia of children's issues worldwide: North Africa and the Middle East* (Vol. 4, pp. 156–161). Westport, CT: Greenwood Press.

Beeman, W.O. (2001). Iran. In C. Ember & M. Ember (Eds.), *Countries and their cultures* (Vol. 2, pp. 1066–1069). New York: Macmillan Reference USA.

Briegel, T. (2008). The United Arab Emirates. In I. Epstein & G. Talhami (Eds.), *The Greenwood encyclopedia of children's issues worldwide: North Africa and the Middle East* (Vol. 4, pp. 313–319). Westport, CT: Greenwood Press.

Chatty, D., & Peterson, J.E. (2001). Oman. In C. Ember & M. Ember (Eds.), *Countries and their cultures* (Vol. 3, pp. 1685–1687). New York: Macmillan.

Cogswell, S.D., & Gerami, S. (2003). Afghanistan. In L. Walter & M. Desai (Eds.), *The Greenwood encyclopedia of women's issues worldwide: Asia and Oceania* (Vol. 1, pp. 12–18). Westport, CT: Greenwood Press.

Cole, D.P. (2001). Saudi Arabia. In C. Ember & M. Ember (Eds.), *Countries and their cultures* (Vol. 4, pp. 1936–1937). New York: Macmillan.

Cunningham, C.E. (2001). Indonesia. In C. Ember & M. Ember (Eds.), *Countries and their cultures* (Vol. 2, pp. 1047–1048). New York: Macmillan Reference USA.

Daadaoui, M. (2008). Oman. In I. Epstein & G. Talhami (Eds.), *The Greenwood encyclopedia of children's issues worldwide: North Africa and the Middle East* (Vol. 4, pp. 177–181). Westport, CT: Greenwood Press.

Daeg de Mott, D.K. (1998a). Afghanis. In T. Gall (Ed.), *Encyclopedia of cultures and daily life: Asia and Oceania* (Vol. 1, pp. 18–22). New York: Worldmark.

Daeg de Mott, D.K. (1998b). Yemenis. In T. Gall (Ed.), *Encyclopedia of cultures and daily life: Asia and Oceania* (Vol. 3, pp. 383–384). New York: Worldmark.

Dahlgren, S. (2003). United Arab Emirates. In B. Sherif-Trask & L. Walter (Eds.), *The Greenwood encyclopedia of women's issues worldwide: North Africa and the Middle East* (Vol. 4, pp. 441–450). Westport, CT: Greenwood Press.

Dalton, W.G. (2001). Libya. In C. Ember & M. Ember (Eds.), *Countries and their cultures* (Vol. 3, pp. 1300–1302). New York: Macmillan Reference USA.

Darwiche, F. (2001). Lebanon. In C. Ember & M. Ember (Eds.), *Countries and their cultures* (Vol. 3, pp. 1270–1271). New York: Macmillan Reference USA.

Davis, S.D., Limansubroto, C.D.M., Piercy, F.P., & Soekandar, A. (2005). Indonesian families. In N. Garcia-Preto, J. Giordano, & M. McGoldrick (Eds.), *Ethnicity & family therapy* (3rd ed., pp. 333–337). New York: The Guilford Press.

DeLong-Bas, N.J. (2008). Saudi Arabia. In I. Epstein & G. Talhami (Eds.), *The Greenwood encyclopedia of children's issues worldwide: North Africa and the Middle East* (Vol. 4, pp. 250–253). Westport, CT: Greenwood Press.

Dwairy, M. (2006). *Counseling and psychotherapy with Arabs and Muslims: A culturally sensitive approach*. New York: Teachers College Press.

Dwairy, M., & Van Sickle, T.D. (1996). Western psychotherapy in traditional Arabic societies. *Clinical Psychology Review, 16*, 231–249. As cited in Haboush, K.L. (2005). Lebanese and Syrian families. In M. McGoldrick, J. Giordano, & N. Garcia-Preto (Eds.), *Ethnicity and family therapy* (3rd ed., pp. 468–486). New York: The Guilford Press.

El-Hassan, K.M. (2008). Sudan. In I. Epstein & L. Arntson (Eds.), *The Greenwood encyclopedia of children's issues worldwide: Sub-Saharan Africa* (Vol. 6, pp. 474–480). Westport, CT: Greenwood Press.

Gerami, S. (2003). Turkey. In J. Ponzetti (Ed.), *International encyclopedia of marriage and family* (Vol. 1, pp. 47–49). New York: Macmillan.

Glascock, A.P. (1998). Somalis. In T. Gall (Ed.), *Encyclopedia of cultures and daily life: Africa* (Vol. 1, pp. 387–389). New York: Worldmark.

Goodnow, J.J., Cashmore, J., Cotton, S., & Knight, R. (1984). Mother's developmental timetables in two cultural groups. *International Journal of Psychology, 19*, 193–206.

Gursoy, A. (2003). Turkey. In J. Ponzetti (Ed.), *International encyclopedia of marriage and family* (Vol. 4, pp. 1670–1673). New York: Macmillan.

Haboush, K.L. (2005). Lebanese and Syrian families. In M. McGoldrick, J. Giordano, & N. Garcia-Preto (Eds.), *Ethnicity and family therapy*. (3rd ed., pp. 468–486). New York: The Guilford Press.

Halim, A.M. (2003). Sudan. In A. Tripp & L. Walter (Eds.), *The Greenwood encyclopedia of women's issues worldwide: Sub-Saharan Africa* (Vol. 6, pp. 439–445). Westport, CT: Greenwood Press.

Harris, M.S. (2001). Bangladesh. In C. Ember & M. Ember (Eds.), *Countries and their cultures* (Vol. 1, pp. 176–177). New York: Macmillan Reference USA.

Hojat, M., & Mehryar, A.H. (2003). Iran. In J.J. Ponzetti (Ed.), *International encyclopedia of marriage and family* (2nd ed., Vol. 2, pp. 949–952). New York: Macmillan.

Hopkins, N.S. (2001). Tunisia. In C. Ember & M. Ember (Eds.), *Countries and their cultures* (Vol. 4, pp. 2252–2255). New York: Macmillan.

Hopkins, N.S., & Saad, R. (2001). Egypt. In C. Ember & M. Ember (Eds.), *Countries and their cultures* (Vol. 2, pp. 684–685). New York: Macmillan Reference USA.

Howard, C. (2001). Pakistan. In C. Ember & M. Ember (Eds.), *Countries and their cultures* (Vol. 3, p. 1698). New York: Macmillan.

Hus, J.A., & Jarchow, E. (2008). Indonesia. In I. Epstein & J. Pattnaik (Eds.), *The Greenwood encyclopedia of children's issues worldwide: Asia and Oceania* (p. 222). Westport, CT: Greenwood Press.

Issitt, M.L. (2008a). Algeria. In I. Epstein & G.H. Talhami (Eds.), *The Greenwood encyclopedia of children's issues worldwide: North Africa and the Middle East* (pp. 8–9). Westport, CT: Greenwood Press.

Issitt, M.L. (2008b). Tunisia. In I. Epstein & G.H. Talhami (Eds.), *The Greenwood encyclopedia of children's issues worldwide: North Africa and the Middle East* (Vol. 4, pp. 296–301). Westport, CT: Greenwood Press.

Jalali, B. (2005). Iranian families. In M. McGoldrick, J. Giordano, & N. Garcia-Preto (Eds.), *Ethnicity and family therapy* (3rd ed., pp. 451–467). New York: The Guilford Press.

Johnston, A.J. (2001). The United Kingdom of Morocco. In C. Ember & M. Ember (Eds.), *Countries and their cultures* (Vol. 3, pp. 1519–1520). New York: Macmillan.

Jones, R. (2008). *Libya*. London: Kuperard.

Kenyon, S.M. (1998). Sudanese. In T. Gall (Ed.), *Encyclopedia of cultures and daily life: Africa* (Vol. 1, pp. 403–404). New York: Worldmark.

Khalaf, S.N. (2001). United Arab Emirates. In C. Ember & M. Ember (Eds.), *Countries and their cultures* (Vol. 4, p. 2328). New York: Macmillan.

King, V.T. (2008). *Malaysia*. London: Kuperard.

Kukreja, S. (2003). Malaysia. In J.J. Ponzetti (Ed.), *International encyclopedia of marriage and family* (2nd ed., Vol. 3, pp. 1067–1069). New York: Macmillan.

Lodrick, D.O. (1998a). Bangladeshis. In T. Gall (Ed.), *Encyclopedia of cultures and daily life: Asia and Oceania* (Vol. 3, p. 91). Detroit: Gale.

Lodrick, D.O. (1998b). Pakistanis. In T. Gall (Ed.), *Encyclopedia of cultures and daily life: Asia and Oceania* (Vol. 3, pp. 614-615). New York: Worldmark.

Loew, H. (2001). Kuwait. In C. Ember & M. Ember (Eds.), *Countries and their cultures* (Vol. 2, pp. 1233–1234). New York: Macmillan Reference USA.

Magnarella, P.J. (2001). Turkey. In C. Ember & M. Ember (Eds.), *Countries and their cultures* (Vol. 4, pp. 2270–2271). New York: Macmillan.

Maravilla, C.S. (2008). Libya. In I. Epstein & G.H. Talhami (Eds.), *The Greenwood encyclopedia of children's issues worldwide: North Africa and the Middle East* (p. 145). Westport, CT: Greenwood Press.

Mehryar, A.H., Ahmad-Nia, S., & Jalali-Savar, A. (2008). Iran. In I. Epstein & G.H. Talhami (Eds.), *The Greenwood encyclopedia of children's issues worldwide: North Africa and the Middle East* (pp. 71–75). Westport, CT: Greenwood Press.

Mensch, B.S., Ibrahim, B.L., Lee, S.M., & El-Gibably, O. (2003). Gender-role attitudes among Egyptian adolescents. *Studies in Family Planning, 34*, 8–18. As cited in Rowe, M., & Rizzo, H. (2008). Egypt. In I. Epstein & G.H. Talhami (Eds.), *The Greenwood encyclopedia of children's issues worldwide: North Africa and The Middle East* (pp. 48–51). Westport, CT: Greenwood Press.

Mesbah, S. & Huda, K.M.S. (2008). Bangladesh. In I. Epstein & J. Pattnaik (Eds.), *The Greenwood encyclopedia of children's issues worldwide: Asia and Oceania* (pp. 34–35). Westport, CT: Greenwood Press.

Monsutti, A. (2001). Afghanistan. In C. Ember & M. Ember (Eds.), *Countries and their cultures* (Vol. 1, pp. 7–9). New York: Macmillan.

Mwaniki, N. (1998). Egyptians. In T. Gall (Ed.), *Encyclopedia of cultures and daily life: Africa* (Vol. 1, pp. 137–139). Detroit: Gale.

Nath, S. (2005). Pakistani families. In N. Garcia-Preto, J. Giordano, & M. McGoldrick (Eds.), *Ethnicity & family therapy* (pp. 414–415). New York: Guilford Press.

Pietanza, E.C. (2001). Iraq. In C. Ember & M. Ember (Eds.), *Countries and their cultures* (Vol. 2, pp. 1085–1087). New York: Macmillan Reference USA.

Rodionov, M. (2001). Yemen. In C. Ember & M. Ember (Eds.), *Countries and their cultures* (Vol. 4, pp. 2459–2460). New York: Macmillan.

Rowe, M., & Rizzo, H. (2008). Egypt. In I. Epstein & G.H. Talhami (Eds.), *The Greenwood encyclopedia of children's issues worldwide: North Africa and the Middle East* (pp. 48–51). Westport, CT: Greenwood Press.

Schmidt, D. (2001). Jordan. In C. Ember & M. Ember (Eds.), *Countries and their cultures* (Vol. 2, pp. 1162–1164). New York: Macmillan Reference USA.

See, C.M. (2008). Malaysia. In I. Epstein & J. Pattnaik (Eds.), *The Greenwood encyclopedia of children's issues worldwide: Asia and Oceania* (pp. 262–263). Westport, CT: Greenwood Press.

Sherif, B. (2003). Egypt. In J.J. Ponzetti (Ed.), *International encyclopedia of marriage and family: Ea-Ju* (2nd ed., pp. 506–510). New York: Macmillan.

Standish, S. (2010). *Syria.* London: Kuperard.

Stanford, E. (2001a). Algeria. In C. Ember & M. Ember (Eds.), *Countries and their cultures* (Vol. 1, pp. 31–32). New York: Macmillan Reference USA.

Stanford, E. (2001b). Sudan. In C. Ember & M. Ember (Eds.), *Countries and their cultures* (Vol. 4, pp. 2106–2109). New York: Macmillan.

Stanford, E. (2001c). Syria. In C. Ember & M. Ember (Eds.), *Countries and their cultures* (Vol. 4, pp. 2155–2156). New York: Macmillan.
Surgin, A.H. (2001). Somalia. In C. Ember & M. Ember (Eds.), *Countries and their cultures* (Vol. 4, pp. 2040–2043). New York: Macmillan.
Tyson, D. (1998). Turks. In T. Gall (Ed.), *Encyclopedia of cultures and daily life: Asia and Oceania* (Vol. 3, pp. 790–792). New York: Worldmark.
Wehbi, S. (2002). "Women with nothing to lose": Marriageability and women's perceptions of rape and consent in contemporary Beirut. *Women's Studies International Forum, 25*, 287–300. doi:http://dx.doi.org/10.1016/S0277-5395(02)00255-8
Williams, S. (2008). *Iran.* London: Kuperard.
Williamson, T. (2001). Malaysia. In C. Ember & M. Ember (Eds.), *Countries and their cultures* (Vol. 3, pp. 1370–1372). New York: Macmillan Reference USA.
Wright, C.I. (2003). United Arab Emirates. In B. Sherif-Trask & L. Walter (Eds.), *The Greenwood encyclopedia of women's issues worldwide: North Africa and the Middle East* (Vol. 4, pp. 413–420). Westport, CT: Greenwood Press.
York, J. (2009). *Morocco.* Rev. London: Kuperard.
Zarr, G. (2009). *Tunisia.* London: Kuperard.

Chapter 3

THE IMPACT OF COLONIALISM

Adequate recognition of many family struggles within the modern Muslim family should begin with an examination of their colonial history along with the impact incurred through the actions of European countries and Russian towards Muslims in the seventeenth, eighteenth, nineteenth, and twentieth centuries. Similar to locating fault lines in order to determine where earthquakes are apt to develop, examining the history of the people affected, particularly who did what to whom, helps explain Muslim family identity and many relational and cultural issues they currently face. It can also explain the animosity between Muslims and the West and the advent of terrorism executed by extreme Islamist groups against generally the West and particularly the United States. This concept is of explicit consequence during therapy with Muslim families because the therapist may harbor stereotypes and categorizations that may in turn be eliminated through an understanding of the relevant colonial history.

The Modern Muslim World after Colonialism

In the nineteenth century, European empires started the conquest of India, continued to part of Africa, and then began the colonization of Muslim territories (Nasr, 2013). The split of Arab states from the Ottoman Empire after World War I was the last part of the colonizers' adventure. Once World War II ended, Britain and then France started withdrawing from many of these territories, and the colonial period officially ended. From 1947 on, Muslim states began to develop, even though some countries like Iran and Afghanistan were never formally colonized and remained independent. The colonial powers had to negotiate withdrawal in places like Malaysia, India, and the Persian Gulf emirates and left after bloody and brutal wars of independence in places like Algeria. However, since Europeans had to safeguard their financial benefits and economic interests after their political and military secessions, the decolonization process was very slow. For example, 1953's military coup in Iran and 1956's military coup in Egypt are great examples of the reaffirmation of the power of the colonialists, even though direct European control and ruling over Muslims ended in this era.

Most Muslim territories from Southeast Asia to sub-Saharan Africa gained independence from colonialism to form independent Muslim countries or became parts of independent non-Muslim countries by the mid-1970s. Considering this timeline, there still exists a considerable Muslim population, from all Muslim countries, who were subject to colonial rule first-hand. Even though the greater population of modern Muslims were born after World War II (and even after 1980), colonization still resonates as a significant impact on their lives in all these countries.

The legacy of colonialism can explain the differences and similarities with state development in the Muslim world. For example, ethnic identity, contextual and religious influences, and social characteristics illuminate the similarities among Muslim countries while leadership and economics explain the differences. However, state formation within the Muslim world can only be explained by the great influence of colonialism. Historically, Muslims have been ruled by virtually all the colonial powers. The British and the French controlled most parts of Muslim territories in Africa, Asia, and the Arab world (Nasr, 2013). Germans, Russians, Portuguese, and Spaniards controlled Muslim territories in Malaysia, East Africa, the Caucasus, the Philippines, and Central Asia, while the Dutch ruled over territories that later became Indonesia (Nasr, 2013). Today, Israel's control of the Gaza Strip and the West Bank is supposedly the last direct colonial control of Muslims' lands. Although the essential characteristics of colonialism were the same in these territories, they differ in how colonial powers and authority were used and utilized in different regions. There are many similarities as well as idiosyncrasies among various Muslim politics based on their histories and, more importantly, their experiences with colonialism. Most importantly, even though the colonial period lasted for less than a century, it changed social relations, politics, geography, and the economy of all the areas it controlled forever. The legacy of colonialism has continued to impact Muslim countries' institutions, economies, and societies. The impact of colonial power dynamics reached far beyond the relationships of political imperialism and economics. It also persisted in terms of ideologies, political visions, and institutions and became a very strong indication for the historic link connecting a past that the new states wanted to desperately distance themselves from and their current so-called independent realities.

Today, the Muslim world comprises many nation-states, but the notion of a national country is fairly new in many parts of the Muslim world. In the pre-modern period Muslims were politically united under the caliphate, sheikhs, and sultanates, who ruled in the name of Islam and were very mindful of regional, ethnic, and linguistic differences among themselves. Thus, it is fair to say that the idea of nationalism brought to this region from the West is the byproduct of colonialism despite the fact that ethnic affiliation and national identity sentiments were always strong even before colonialism. For example, Iranians historically viewed themselves as different from Turks and Arabs, and the birth of Shi'ism in Iran can be linked to Iranians trying to mark their national identity, separating them from Arabs, and define their religious identity, separating them from the Turks, who are mostly Sunni. Ethnic nationalism, however, has its origins in the colonial period and is new to the Muslim world. Colonial powers made nationalism a primary form of political identity and made it more important than Islamic identity, and over time nationalism developed and became part of Muslim political consciousness.

The legacy of colonialism in the Middle East has been full of conflicts. First, many of the state divisions by the colonial powers created problems. Some divisions were arbitrarily and only accommodated the colonial power without any regard for their impact on resources and peoples. Other divisions were made only because the colonialists needed to solve political conflicts among themselves and create safeguards against other colonialists or to placate other unhappy European colonizers (Nasr, 2013).

Economic interests and strategic decisions also led to the formation of new colonial states. For example, Britain wanted to have access to oil in the Persian Gulf, which made the formation of Kuwait possible; years later, the same interests in oil led Britain to discourage Brunei from merging with Malaysia. France created Lebanon, which was part of Syria, in order to create a Christian-Arab state. Jordan was created because King Abdullah helped the British during World War I and his family felt deceived by the way the Arab lands of the Ottoman Empire were divided among European powers (Nasr, 2013).

Therefore, in actuality, colonialism molded the way Muslims perceived their own politics and identities and divided the routes by which each Muslim country adapted after their independence. This is particularly important because all the rulers after independence were elites educated in Europe and trained to serve European powers. Western political and economic models substituted for the Islamic political and economic systems, creating overcrowded cities, increased joblessness, corrupted governments, and a growing gap amid the rich and poor. Thus, instead of helping Islamic states have a better quality of life, Westernization collapsed traditional social, religious, and family values.

Today, corrupted government officials, mostly kings or military or ex-military officers who were not democratically elected, rule the majority of countries in the Muslim world. Government security forces, military, and police control these countries, and freedoms of speech, assembly, and press are relentlessly restricted. These states function under authoritarian regimes that are opposed to civil society and a free press. Most importantly, not only Europe, and later the US, are influencing those who came to power in Muslim states; they also have strong partnerships with totalitarian governments. The European and US governments accept and support these unelected and undemocratic governments to ensure and in exchange for Western access to oil and many other natural resources.

In addition, commitments to keeping the borders between these states and creating nationalism were emphasized. National identities based on being Syrian or Iraqi became important, and Syrian and Iraqi officials, for example, who under the Ottoman Empire operated based on the same social, political, and literary culture, now established connections to different European languages and traditions and became completely separated. These different political and administrative ties, therefore, helped strengthen nationalisms and broke the strong bond and connection with other Muslims living in neighboring countries.

In many situations, however, colonial authorities created borders and used nationalism to separate people but did not unify those who lived within the boundaries of a unified country. In fact, in many instances, they did precisely the opposite. They maintained control by encouraging competition and clashes between religious, ethnic, tribal, and linguistic groups. Therefore, conflicts and tensions between peoples living in the same country who have not integrated into one state have triggered lots of challenges to protecting countries' borders. Some examples are religious and ethnic conflicts in countries like Nigeria, Pakistan, and Malaysia; tensions in Lebanon; and the continuing Kurdish quandary in Iran, Iraq, and Turkey. These represent a subcategory of all the problems created by state formation on the basis of colonial decisions for segregation. It is such that, when we ask why the majority of Muslim countries are so affected by political unrest and continuous violence, the answer is the colonial intrusion, both past and present, within this whole region. Consequently, Muslim families' traditions, customs, and belief systems have been devalued and degraded to the extent that a transition has been made from the physical colonization of their land to the psychological colonization of their minds.

Colonized Mind

After 1945 and many movements towards 'independence,' the Western colonial powers physically and visibly left Muslim countries. However, the colonial systems for science, health, technology, law, education, and many other things ensured that these formerly colonized people supposedly would not advance in ways different from what the colonizers had envisioned for them so that the 'third world' would continue its subordination to the Western world. The continuation of policies, economic dependencies, and ways of life that were originally forced upon the 'third world' when they were directly colonized is called 'mental colonization.' Fanon (1961) believes that mental colonization is very powerful because colonized people sustain and maintain their colonization by continuing to imitate the cultural ideals of those who colonized and oppressed them. Jalal Al-e Ahmad in his classic book *Occidentosis* (1984) examines mental colonialism and states that people from the 'third world' have been influenced and even infected by a disorder that makes them obsessed and captivated with the West while losing connection to their own culture, traditions, and outlook.

CLINICAL IMPLICATIONS

Today, colonialism has become a bad word, but in our everyday reality the world remains entangled in the relationship between domination and exploitation using an innovative name: 'globalization.' The same 1% of the world's population still continue to dominate the other 99%, which is very similar to the arrangements colonialists had but with a fancier and more sophisticated title that fools many into thinking this new arrangement is more democratic and egalitarian than the previous one.

As has been discussed in this chapter, colonialism has influenced not just politics and economics, but also Muslim families' consciousness. Therefore, they perceive their relationship satisfaction, parenting styles, marital intimacy, friendships, and any other relational issues through a Westernized lens in order to measure their happiness. Consequently, clinicians need to be aware of the influence of colonization on Muslim families' minds and pay more attention to the way individuals, couples, and families describe their relational difficulties. It is also imperative for practitioners to understand how Western models have been used to recolonize the minds and souls of Muslim families and reexamine their own values and biases when they come to describe healthy family functioning.

REFERENCES

Ahmad, J.A. (1984). *Occidentosis, a plague from the west.* Berkeley: Mizan Press.

Fanon, F. (1961). *The wretched of the earth* (*Les Damnés de la Terre*). New York: Grove Press.

Nasr, S.V. (2013). European colonialism and the emergence of modern Muslim states. In J.L. Esposito (Ed.), *Oxford Islamic studies online: The Oxford history of Islam.* Retrieved from www.oxfordislamicstudies.com/article/book/islam-9780195107999/islam-9780195107999-chapter-13

Chapter 4

GENDER AND POWER

Discourses about power and gender relations in Islam have been part of many debates over the centuries, but the development of a specific interest in learning about Muslim cultures in general and about gender dynamics in particular is part of the modern-day encounter of the West, Islam, and Muslim societies. It is apparent that the imbalanced and unequal relationship between men and women in Muslim societies is the reason for a lot of attention at different levels such as academic, social, and developmental. Many researchers and scholars claim that the imbalanced relationship between men and women and the lack of improvement in inequality in gender relations is a consequence of the influences of Islamic ideology. Nonetheless, restricting and using Islam as the only reason for discrimination against women is superficial at best and in many instances may be a major contributor to these inequalities instead of creating a way for challenging and removing them. Thus, it is imperative that gender relationship analysis be at the multidimensional and multidisciplinary level in order to reach an optimum level of understanding about gender dynamics in Muslim societies.

There are many important questions that can be raised about the role of Islam in defining the status of women in Muslim societies. We can ask if it is the religion itself, or a male, patriarchal-based interpretation of it, that affects women's place in these societies and if there are other related factors affecting and reinforcing this status. It is also equally imperative to examine how in these cultural contexts we can find some incentives for change and social development in creating a gender-just society.

Stowasser (1984) argues that if we stay within the religious texts and frameworks, even though there are verses that discuss dissimilarities between men and women, "woman's essential equality with man is more complete in Islam than it is in Judaism and Christianity" (p. 21). She further explains that "this level of diminished equality stems from the treatment by the two religions of Eve as transgressor, cursing her before Adam, while according to the Koran Adam and Eve were portrayed as transgressors jointly held responsible for mortal sin" (p. 22).

Despite this strong argument, today we see a strong dogmatism and traditionalism in many Islamic societies that has severely exceeded many legal and relational rights established for women in early Islam. The deterioration in the position of women, and consequently the inadequate and imbalanced treatment and restriction of her space, is due to specific interpretation (by men) that has created the current patriarchal societies instead of getting rid of these inequalities. Thus, in light of these religious interpretations (known as *Tafseer*), more restriction were reinforced through history. Stowasser (1984) endorses this problem and states, "The process of progressive exclusion and increasing restrictions imposed on women was clearly visible through comparison of the original Quranic legislation with the series of commentaries which later ages produced" (p. 22). This trend also happened with the Hadiths such that "the later the source, the more abundant, detailed and normative-restrictive the information on women it contains" (p. 23).

Many believe that the Quranic verses have contributed to better status for women compared with the pre-Islamic period, despite men's strong tendency towards a patriarchal model of roles played in families. Thus, even though, compared to other religions, Islam was more advanced in terms of its treatment of women, even within the boundaries of its own basic ideology, Islam has become more conservative and static towards women's liberation and emancipation. A strictly male-dominated interpretation of the Quran and the creation of a legal system based on these interpretations have over time contributed to this rigid and static institutionalization of patriarchy and gender inequality in Muslim societies.

Thus, when considering the current social realities in most Muslim countries, the impact of Islamic history in shaping the status of women becomes the central theme. Mernissi (1996) states that Islam, similar to Christianity and Judaism, "prefers a model of hierarchical relationships and sexual inequality" (p. 14). Thus, it seems like Islam has contributed and reinforced the patriarchal foundations that existed in Arab society before Islam. It seems also that Islam incorporated many other cultural characteristics while spreading the Islamic Empire that allowed "sexual inequality to reassert itself" (p. 69). Thus, the Golden Age of Islam also correlates with patriarchal social and ruling order.

However, we cannot ignore the crucial role of the modern historical experience of Muslim societies, particularly their colonial and nationalist experiences. In this regards, Kandiyoti (1991) states that "an adequate analysis of the position of women in Muslim societies must be grounded in a detailed examination of the political projects of contemporary states and of their historical transformations" (p. 2).

Western Colonialist Construction of 'Muslim Women'

The nineteenth century has been marked as a time of global societal changes that challenged and questioned the religious and social basis of all human societies, and this trend still continues to this day. Western colonialists utilized ideological issues related to politics and economics as their major sources for influencing the Islamic world. The steady and successful development of the worldwide economy and the political superiority of Western countries influenced a global trend that non-Western nations could not circumvent or avoid. These political and economic changes have undeniably been multifaceted, from creating national states in the Middle East to making significant educational reforms. One of the major elements that endured a fundamental alteration in the Islamic world has been the relationship between the sexes. Muslim women started to search for their identity in society at the same time that Islamic scholars were writing about female sexuality being a potent and aggressive force with the potential for creating social chaos. Many secular feminists claim that this rigid Islamic interpretation has been the reason for practices that have traditionally symbolized women's forced seclusion to the private sphere, like veiling, and extreme resistance to allow and welcome women to the university and the workplace (Ahmed, 1992; Mernissi, 1996; Moghissi, 1999). Modernity, which was imposed by colonialists, was perceived by hegemonic Muslim (male) interests as a threat because it was a force changing and renegotiating spatial (public/private) boundaries.

It is not surprising, then, that Western colonizers used the role and status of the Muslim woman in Islamic societies to achieve one of their many imperialistic goals. For example, Lord Cromer, who was the British consul general in Egypt from 1883 to 1907, is the classic example of such a colonizer. Cromer was convinced that the Islamic religion and their way of life was inferior, but his main criticism was about Islam's treatment of women (Ahmed, 1992). Lord Cromer declared that the Islamic way of treating women, and insisting on veiling and secluding them, was the "fatal obstacle" to the Egyptian's "attainment of that elevation of thought and character which should accompany the introduction of Western civilization" (Moghissi, 1999, p. 37). Lord Cromer insisted that Egyptians must be "persuaded or forced" to turn into "civilized" people by getting rid of the veil (Moghissi, 1999). Thus, "unveiling women became a stick with which the West could beat the East" (Malti-Douglas, 1991, p.174). The Muslim woman was to be exploited by the Western man but protected from enslavement by the Muslim man. She was to be liberated from her own ignorance and her culture's cruelty (Moghissi, 1999). On the other hand, Muslim men viewed hiding women from the gaze of Western viewers and protecting their bodies and minds against these transformations as safeguarding their Islamic identity, collective pride, and social and cultural stability (Moghissi, 1999). Thus, it is possible to say that perhaps the resistance of Islamic societies to alter their perceptions about women's status was the reaction of a culture that had been stereotyped and made to feel inferior for its treatment of women. Hence, in this view, "it was colonialism which made the Muslim woman and her rights central to its imperial policy in the Middle East" (Moghissi, 1999, p. 39), and it was Islamic conservatism that continued to embrace women's subjugated status. For instance, Moghissi argues:

> In the end, ironically, Islamic fundamentalism, by embracing the female body as the symbolic representation of communal dignity, and by drawing only on the Qur'an and orthodox texts to explain, as divine, the historically developed subjugation of women in Islamic societies, recycle the totalizing colonial conception of Islam and women's rights as a static, unchanging and unchangeable order. As with other forms of extremism, the two opposing poles end up on the same side on certain important issues. By manipulating the female body as a playing card in oppositional politics,

> fundamentalists, in fact, embrace, however unsought and uncomfortable, the views of the Western colonizer.
>
> (Moghissi, 1999, p. 30)

This discourse about the equivalency of being veiled and oppressed and about the urgency of emancipating the claustrophobic heads of Muslim women from their burdening fabric continues to be part of many major debates.

WHITE WESTERN FEMINIST CONSTRUCTIONS OF 'MUSLIM WOMEN'

White Western feminist discussions about women in the third world are full of charges of colonialism, universalism and misinterpretation of the third-world women's experiences because these discussions basically eradicate the cultural differences that differentiate all of our experiences from each other (Aguilar, 1997; Mohanty, 1995; Sandoval, 2000). It constructs all of us third-world women, irrespective of our culture and national origin, as a collective "us" contrasted with the white Western women's "them" (Mohanty, 1995).

This is what many 'third-world' women find problematic in white Western feminist scholarship about Muslim women because it tends to regard third-world women as an ahistorical group and homogenous in terms of other factors like ethnicity, class, and geographical location. Our identities are understood and created before placing us in many of our social institutions like our families and societies. Gender is then perceived to be the main source of our oppression, instead of oppression producing specific forms of gender relations. White Western feminists have used a model of subjectivity that does not allow for appropriate and adequate agency in any of us 'third-world women.'

Nevertheless, the white Western feminist perception of Muslim women was not created in a vacuum. There has been a secular feminist movement in Muslim countries that emerged from third-world women's own willing participation in being viewed as modern with all its hegemonic first-world formations and colonial discourses. In their attempts to free themselves from the oppression placed on them by Islamic conservative perspectives, secular third-world feminists joined white Western feminists in describing the fellow veiled third-world woman as having many "needs" or "problems," but few having any "choices" or the freedom to make decisions and act (Mohanty, 1995, p. 45). This participation consciously or unconsciously led to the exploitation, subjugation, and oppression of many women who were struggling to deal with the contradictions of being placed between the imperialism of modernity and narrow-mindedness of tradition (Aguilar, 1997). In order to understand these contradictions, we have to examine the way that modernity is produced in different cultures and in various settings and how the concept of modernity has been disseminated, received, circulated, distributed, received, and even co-modified. There have also been dichotomies created by defining the basic concepts of what is modern only in contrast to what is traditional. As a result, many Muslim women's movements do not get acknowledged partly due to the tendency to judge modernity by dress, sect, or language. For example, a woman who is dressed fashionably in European modern clothes and has a consumerist lifestyle and is submissive in her marital relationship is still seen as modern because she speaks Western languages and has knowledge of Western costume. However, her less-affluent counterpart who wears the *hijab*, speaks only Arabic, and works in an agricultural field or in a factory, but perhaps has joined an underground movement against the Israeli occupation and has a high level of independence and political awareness, is still perceived as backward because of her dress, appearance, and language. Post-modern family therapy should be based on fighting against this definition of modernity that creates a dichotomous and conventional view of a Muslim woman as being secluded, uneducated, and controlled if she chooses to wear *hijab*.

Post-Modern View of Muslim Women

For many years now the majority of Muslim countries have struggled to retrieve their own true identity and escape from the effects of colonialism. Many Muslim-majority societies are desperate for political and social change and want to establish a democratic system in which citizens can elect government officials to represent them and to get rid of pro-Western and authoritarian governments and monarchies. However, any political initiatives such as electing government officials who are not pro-West, or moving towards economic self-sufficiency based on Islamic principles or socialism, are opposed by the West. On the other hand, any social initiatives from the West, feminism, or liberalism threaten the politics of the

East and are rejected by strict Muslim leaders, authoritarian governments, and traditionalists. All these battles, cultural and political, consistently end up impacting Muslim women and their status and rights. A good example is the Islamic revolution in Iran, which overthrew the pro-Western monarchy and created the professed Islamic republic. The new system was openly against Westernization at the same time that it closed many doors to women by a political system with overly misogynous policies. Nevertheless, Iranian women made impressive progress in terms of their relational dynamics with men, social relations in their communities, and political advancements with the government, but in the US media they were portrayed as ineffective and powerless (Daneshpour, 2009).

Further, it is important to realize that the causes of socialization process and change in Muslim societies, both modern and traditional, are complex, dynamic, and delicate, and they need to be understood in their own context. There are many modern influences that we need to take into consideration, including modern education, the public media, the state, and modern art and literature as well as the postcolonial policies of ruling elites who are under direct influences of the Western superpowers. There are other factors influencing the society either directly or indirectly, like economic pressure and emigration, which influence family interactions. In any society where the formal structures of traditionalism are challenged and changing, new ways of thinking surface, and usually the family is at the heart of being affected by all the changes. Therefore, it is within the family unit that these transformations need to be reinforced so that change can happen.

Clinical Implications

There is no question that inequality and discrimination against women in Islamic countries as perpetuated by the system of patriarchal power exist in many Muslim communities. There has been more than enough religious and spiritual preaching about Islam's great respect for equality of women (in an ideal world) and certainly not enough challenges against the injustices executed in Muslim societies. In the beginning, Islam was the most radical and progressive source of liberalization of women's rights in the civilized world. But now, centuries later, much of the Islamic world has lost touch with its cathartic roots and has been responsible for many fundamental abuses of women's rights. Nevertheless, the colonial perception and conceptualization of Islam as a rigid religion and Muslim women's rights as a static and unchangeable reality, along with the white Western feminist monolithic image of Muslim women as passive, powerless, backward, uneducated, and victimized, have simply been fuel to the fire of challenges that Muslim women face.

It is such that, over time, many Muslim women have realized they have been used by colonialists, misunderstood by postcolonialists, undervalued by most Western feminists, and controlled by Islamists—all while they have been busy raising their families and contributing to their societies. Thus, it is important to acknowledge that women have always suffered the consequences of gender inequalities and that politics are often shaped by specific historical, political, and cultural contexts. Thus, women are still painfully situated in an awkward place between Islamists trying to control them and neo-colonial oppressors trying to emancipate them. They are struggling to stay connected to the sphere of family while latching onto the broader sphere of professional life with all its contradictions and challenges.

It is commonly assumed that due to the dominance of Islam and its homogenizing influence on the development and structures of different societies, Muslim societies have a cultural specificity. This specificity is because of the fact that Islam as a religion has a lot to say about the importance of the family and its link to a healthy Muslim community and perceives family to be at the center of both Islam as a faith and community. The other main issue is that the family is viewed as the main social unit maintaining gender relations and sex role differentiation.

Therefore, when working with Muslim families, asking relevant questions and avoiding pitfalls when addressing the question of gender are sustainable and viable ways of understanding gender dynamics. We need to pay more attention to specific issues Muslim families may be dealing with and try to understand particular gender relation patterns in each family as opposed to looking for a generalized pattern based on all the common stereotypes for Muslim families.

References

Aguilar, D.D. (1997). Lost in translation: Western feminism and Asian women. In S. Shall (Ed.), *Dragon ladies: Asian American feminists breathe fire* (pp. 153–165). Boston: South End Press.

Ahmed, L. (1992). *Women and gender in Islam: Historical roots of a modern debate.* New Haven: Yale University Press.
Daneshpour, M. (2009). Steadying the tectonic plates: On being Muslim, feminist academic, and family therapist. In K. Allen, A. Few, & S. Lloyd. (Eds.), *Handbook of feminist family studies* (pp. 340–351). Thousand Oaks, CA: Sage Publications.
Kandiyoti, D. (1991). Introduction. In D. Kandiyoti (Ed.), *Women, Islam and the state* (pp. 1–21). London: Macmillan Press.
Malti-Douglas, F. (1991). *Women's body, women's world: Gender and discourse in Arab Islamic writing.* Princeton, NJ: Princeton University Press.
Mernissi, F. (1996). *Women's rebellion and Islamic memory.* London: Zed Books.
Moghissi, H. (1999). *Feminism and Islamic fundamentalism: The limits of postmodern analysis.* New York: Zed Books.
Mohanty, C.T. (1995). Under Western eyes: Feminist scholarship and colonial discourses. In B. Ashcroft, G. Griffiths, & H. Tiffin (Eds.), *The postcolonial studies reader* (pp. 259–263). London: Routledge.
Sandoval, C. (2000). *Methodology of the oppressed.* Minneapolis: University of Minnesota Press.
Stowasser, B. (1984). The status of women in early Islam. In F. Hussein (Ed.), *Muslim women* (pp. 11–43). New York: St. Martin's Press.

Part II

Family Therapy Theories

Chapter 5

FAMILY THERAPY ASSESSMENT

While it is not possible to claim that all family treatment must follow a universal and chronological pattern, there are commonalities that can help the therapist working with Muslim families maintain objectivity and provide directions for the family. Typically there are four major stages for family therapy that can be used cross-culturally: 1) the preparation stage, which includes mutual acceptance of the definition of the problem and formulation of goals; 2) the evaluation stage, which includes assessment formulation and alliance building; 3) the treatment stage, which includes creating a treatment plan and the managing of resistance; and 4) the termination stage, which includes discussing the termination process and defining the duration and format of the ending. There are important tasks that must be accomplished at each stage before continuing to the next stage. It is important to complete these tasks in each stage for a strong and successful family therapy process.

Stage 1: Preparation

The main tasks of the first stage of family therapy are planning whom to invite to sessions and what kinds of questions to ask. An intake interview should collect enough information about the specific features of the case. Once the therapist knows more about the family dynamics she can decide whom to invite to the sessions. For instance, if concerns are about a child's sleeping, bedwetting, behavioral issues, or mood swings it is appropriate to only request parents and the child to attend the session. In some other situations, when siblings or extended family conflict are part of the problem, then all siblings and extended family members need to be invited to the session.

In the preparation stage, depending on the problem posed by the family and the family therapist's initial hypothesis, the therapist can ask about the family's main concerns and each individual's level of involvement in solving the problem.

Family therapists don't usually have a complete understanding of the presenting problems prior to having explicit information about the family's functioning. It is important to note that this becomes more complicated for Muslim families because they may be even more reluctant to provide straightforward information to the therapist, who is considered an outsider. Therefore, it may take several sessions for therapists to develop a hypothesis as they continue to ask questions and gain more knowledge. For any individual, couple, or family problems, many schools of family therapy can be used to assess the family interactional patterns sustaining the problem, the restricting beliefs about the impact of the problem and each family member's role, and the historical and contextual factors reinforcing the existence of these problems. Some of the typical assessment techniques that can be used with Muslim families are outlined in the following.

Stage 2: Evaluation

The second stage of the family therapy process includes several tasks: creating a contract for evaluation, managing engagement challenges, questioning about the presenting problem, constructing a genogram, and building a working alliance with the family.

Evaluation Contract

Contracting for evaluation includes: making therapeutic expectations clear; reaching a working agreement together; and outlining what the evaluation involves. The interview processes and their duration need to be described. Then the family members are invited to share their views about the presenting problem: how they understand it; what they think makes the problem better or worse; which family member is most affected by it; what solutions they have used prior to coming to therapy; and how they think the issue should be solved. Family therapists must consider the fact that family members may be reluctant to offer information in front of other family members and may try to be respectful to their family hierarchy. Therefore, gaining enough information for further intervention may take longer.

It is imperative, in the evaluation meeting, to highlight the limits of confidentiality and the voluntary participation in therapy since the concept of confidentiality may be viewed differently in Eastern/collectivistic societies, which the majority of Muslims are from. In Eastern cultures, families are less inclined to share information about family issues with outsiders and prefer to rely on other family members to resolve their problems. Therefore, if they make a decision to see a professional outside of their family network, it is crucial for them to fully understand issues related to confidentiality and how the sessions' contents are confidential unless a family member shows signs of being a severe threat to him- or herself or others. It is imperative to discuss with Muslim families believing in extreme relational loyalty that if the therapist decides to breach confidentiality, it is to protect family members from harming themselves or others and not to create bigger problems for the family. For example, in case of suicidal ideations or child abuse, confidentiality may be breached to protect the individual depending on the country's laws and regulations.

Children and teenagers usually have many misconceptions about the nature of therapy and may come to the session assuming that, since they are in trouble with the family, they will be sent to a detention center, be admitted to a hospital, or have to deal with some coercive procedures. It is extremely essential to reassure children and teenagers that attending sessions is voluntary, that the goal is to make everyone feel better, and that there is no coercion involved.

A consent form that covers most of this information is necessary and must be signed before treatment starts (see Figure 5.1). Family members who can read and sign the consent form may be given the form at the beginning of the first session. Therapists can read the consent form to those who cannot read before asking them to sign it.

FAMILY THERAPY INFORMATION AND CONSENT FORM

Welcome! This document contains important information about my professional services and business policies. Please read it carefully and jot down any questions you might have so that we can discuss them at our next meeting. When you sign this document, it will represent an agreement between us.

FAMILY THERAPY SERVICES

Psychotherapy is not easily described in general statements. It varies depending on the personalities of the therapist and client and the particular problems you bring forward. There are many different methods I may use to deal with the problems that you hope to address. Psychotherapy is not like a medical doctor visit. Instead, it calls for a very active effort on your part. In order for the therapy to be most successful, you will have to work on things we talk about both during our sessions and at home.

Psychotherapy can have benefits and risks. Since therapy often involves discussing unpleasant aspects of your life, you may experience uncomfortable feelings like sadness, guilt, anger, frustration, loneliness, and helplessness. On the other hand, psychotherapy has also been shown to have benefits for people who go through it. Therapy often leads to better relationships, solutions to specific problems, and significant reductions in feelings of distress.

Therapy involves a large commitment of time, money, and energy, so you should be very careful about the therapist you select. If you have questions about my procedures, we should discuss them whenever they arise. If your doubts persist, I will be happy to help you set up a meeting with another mental health professional for a second opinion.

MEETINGS

I normally conduct an evaluation and assessment that will last from one to two sessions. During this time, we can both decide if I am the best person to provide the services you need in order to meet your treatment goals. If psychotherapy is begun, I will schedule 50-minute sessions (one appointment 'hour' equals 50 minutes duration) with you at an interval of frequency that is mutually agreed upon.

Figure 5.1: Family therapy information and consent form

PROFESSIONAL FEES

My hourly fee is _______. In addition to scheduled appointments, I charge this amount for other professional services you may need, although I will break down the hourly cost if I work for periods of less than one hour.

BILLING AND PAYMENTS

You will be expected to pay for each session at the time it is held, unless we agree otherwise or unless you have insurance coverage that requires another arrangement. Payment schedules for other professional services will be agreed to when they are requested. (In circumstances of unusual financial hardship, I may be willing to negotiate a fee adjustment or payment installment plan.)

MISSED APPOINTMENTS

Once an appointment hour is scheduled, a block of time is reserved for you. If you need to cancel an appointment, **please provide over one full business day advance notice of cancellation**. For example, if your appointment is scheduled for a Thursday, please call on Wednesday for the following Thursday time, so I have time on Wednesday to contact another client. If you fail to provide proper notice or miss an appointment, **you will be charged at the usual rate. Insurance carriers do not reimburse for such charges.**

CONFIDENTIALITY

Your privacy is very important to me. Additionally, my professional code of ethics and various laws ensure that all conversations you have with me will be held in strictest confidence. However, there are some exceptions to this rule, and you need to be aware that I may or must share information with other agencies or individuals under the following circumstances:

1. When you sign a release of information form that gives me authorization to do so.
2. When I am court ordered to do so.

Figure 5.1: (Continued)

3. When I am required by law to do so, as in the instances of threats of harm to self or others or when there are indications of child neglect, physical or sexual abuse, or abuse of a vulnerable adult.
4. For purposes of billing and accounting related to your services. I may use a billing service to process claims that you and/or your insurance company want me to file for you.
5. If you file a malpractice suit against me, I will be permitted by the courts to reveal information about your therapy.
6. If you disclose information about a physician or certain other licensed healthcare professionals, regarding possible ethical violations, which could lead to disciplinary action by their respective licensing boards.
7. Lastly, the law imposes a limit on the right of privacy with minors with respect to any communication your minor children may have with me. Thus, certain information your child shares with me may also be shared with you. Under some circumstances, the information may not be shared with the parent.

While this written summary of exceptions to confidentiality should prove helpful in informing you about potential problems, it is important that we discuss any questions or concerns that you may have at our next meeting.

I may occasionally find it helpful to consult other professionals about a case. During a consultation, I make every effort to avoid revealing the identity of my client. The consultant is also legally bound to keep the information confidential. If you don't object, I will not tell you about these consultations unless I feel that it is important to our work together.

FAMILY THERAPY WITH CHILDREN

If the main problem involves your children, parents are invited. We find that it is most helpful if the young person with the problem and both parents attend the appointments. Fathers (or step-fathers) have a particularly important contribution to make to our understanding of young people's problems and to their resolution.

Figure 5.1: (Continued)

COUPLE THERAPY

If the main problem involves an adult in the family or if there are marital difficulties, it is most helpful if both partners attend the appointments.

As indicated by my signature below, I have read and understand all of the information contained in this document.

Client Signature: ______________________________
Printed Name: ______________________________
Date: ______________________________

Figure 5.1: (Continued)

Managing Engagement Challenges

During the evaluation stage, there may be some challenges that the family therapist has to resolve. For example, key family members may not want to participate; the referral source may have given inaccurate information about the family; and children may feel suspicious of the therapy process and decide not to engage.

It is very common in all cultures, Muslim families included, for the mother to take the responsibility for seeking help for children or marital issues without involving the father, which may indicate that the father is not interested in being part of the therapy process. It is important not to make this a patriarchal gender-specific issue and ask the family members who attend the session to invite other family members because change is longer lasting when all members take responsibility for their contributions to the problem and the solution. In case of any key family members including the father not wanting to participate, it is important to send a message to them specifying that you are very interested in hearing their perspective because it helps you formulate a hypothesis regarding family dynamics and help the attending family members change. The absent or reluctant family member usually shows up and joins in the therapy process because he/she feels that his/her views are important and respected.

In case of having inaccurate information from the referral source, it is essential for the therapist to formulate hypotheses based on the information family members provide and see the family in a new light. If therapists are working with immigrant Muslim families living in the West, it is important to know that Muslim family values are generally pathologized and taken out of context; thus, families may get stuck with the way they are perceived and act accordingly. Therefore, concentrating on family strengths and challenges they have faced helps the therapist form better alliances and become more successful in helping the family change.

In case of children not wanting to engage and participate in family therapy and who feel pressured to be at the session, we can invite them to observe the discussion between parents and therapist without being forced to participate. The therapist then can ask parents to speculate about their children's perspectives in front of them while they are observing, and children may join in the dialogue to discuss their perspectives about their parents' assumptions and opinions while remaining respectful to their parents.

Presenting Problem

Family members should feel comfortable discussing their perspectives about the presenting problem after the initial evaluation and having established a sense of trust. Therapists may ask questions regarding the frequency and intensity of the problematic behaviors; all previous attempts to solve the problems; family members' understanding about the causes of these problems; and possible resolutions they want to explore. While carefully listening and asking for more details about the social context of the problems, the therapist needs to pay particular attention to possible interactional patterns that are maintaining the problems. Some useful questions that can be asked are:

Everyone has a perception of family issues. Can you tell us how you see it?
How do you think these family issues began?
What do you think is going on right now?
Can you describe a specific incident that happened recently?
What makes the situation better or worse?
What solutions have been tried?
Were any of the solutions helpful?
What do you think will happen if the problem does not get solved soon?
If the problem gets solved soon, what do you think has been helpful?

Constructing a Genogram

A genogram is a detailed demonstration of a family tree that displays the interaction of several generations within a family. It allows the user to analyze family, emotional, and social relationships within a group. It is used to recognize recurring patterns of behavior and identify hereditary tendencies. It is highly recommended that a genogram be constructed in the first few family assessment sessions. Genogram symbols are presented in Figure 5.2, 5.3, and 5.4, and areas that need to be covered in genogram construction can be found in Table 5.1.

It is always beneficial to create the genogram with family members present in the session so they can see it as it is drawn. A large piece of paper or a whiteboard may be used to draw the genogram. When constructing

Table 5.1: Information to include in genograms

Demographics	• Name • Age • Job and education
Life Cycle Transitions	• Births and deaths • Marital relationships • Changing living arrangements • Leaving home • Returning home • Anniversaries of individual and family transitions • Religious ceremonies and transitions
Protective Factors	• Successful problem resolutions • Education and job performance • Good connection with friends, family members, society • Leisure activities, sport • Exceptional personal achievements • Relying on higher power (God) • Positive personal traits
Risk Factors	• Illnesses and hospitalizations • Mental health issues • Drug and alcohol abuse • Temper control, abuse and violence, unlawful behaviors • Fears, guilt, stigmas
Dyadic Relationship	• Supportive partnership and coalitions • Stressors and conflicts
Triadic Relationship	• Triangulation (a child is expected to take sides with parents or other family members) • Unreasonable triangles with cross-generational coalitions • Detouring—due to child's behavioral problems, parents join together and express anger at the child • Detouring—due to child's emotional problems, parents join together and express concerns for the child

Multigenerational Complexity	• Multigenerational dyadic relationship patterns (e.g., mother-in-law and daughter-in-law have conflictual relationships) • Multigenerational triadic relationship patterns (e.g., triangulation occurs in more than one generation)

a genogram, make sure to go through the process slowly because it may be difficult for Muslims with collectivistic cultural values to share too many details to someone outside their family network at the beginning of the therapy process. Further, it is important to note that since Muslim families' typical gender relationship patterns prohibit boys and girls being raised together, and family interrelationships are vital to many families' survival, it is common for first, second, or distant cousin to marry each other. If the Muslim family is working with a Western therapist, they may feel embarrassed to discuss these relationships, fearing that the therapist will judge them negatively. Therefore, the therapist should make sure not to use a judgmental tone when family members are talking about these marriages. It is also vital not to ask too many specific questions about negative events or insignificant details. Genogram construction can be a chance to discuss family members' strengths, asking them about relational patterns between significant family members. There may be times that family members cannot remember specific details about ages, dates, occupations, or some other details, and it is appropriate to ignore these details if the therapist doesn't think it represents a significant pattern.

Genogram construction gives us a chance to identify and discuss family members' strengths. Ask family members to identify and discuss positive traits for each family member. This type of identification helps raise morale, diminish hopelessness, and allow families to develop a more hopeful perspective about themselves.

Although it is important to spend time asking questions about strengths, inquiring about vulnerabilities, illnesses, and adjustment problems should be brief. One way to accomplish this is by asking the question about each generation instead of each individual in the family.

Inquiring about complicated multigenerational patterns and triangles may be accomplished by asking questions about coalitions. This task can be accomplished by asking each family member to state who in the family they think is the closest to another member and who has more conflicts with other members. Further, asking about similarities between relationships in different generations can identify multigenerational patterns. Significant supportive or not very supportive individuals in the family's social system can also be identified and included in the genogram. Muslim family relationships tend to be more intertwined, and extended family members, especially in-laws, have important contributions to nuclear family decision-making processes. Therefore, it is crucial to ask questions related to these significant interactions and the consequences for each family member. Life cycle transitions are an important part of family life, and questions regarding how each member has handled developmental issues should be asked. More questions about the management of specific life cycle stages and transitions from one stage to another are important to evaluate especially because the younger generation in Muslim families is supposed to provide care and assistance to the older generation.

Other assessment tools, in addition to genograms, may provide us with information regarding the strengths and weaknesses of each family member; options include assessment tools that are culturally sensitive for each cultural group and can be used to assess the overall functioning of families in different cultural groups.

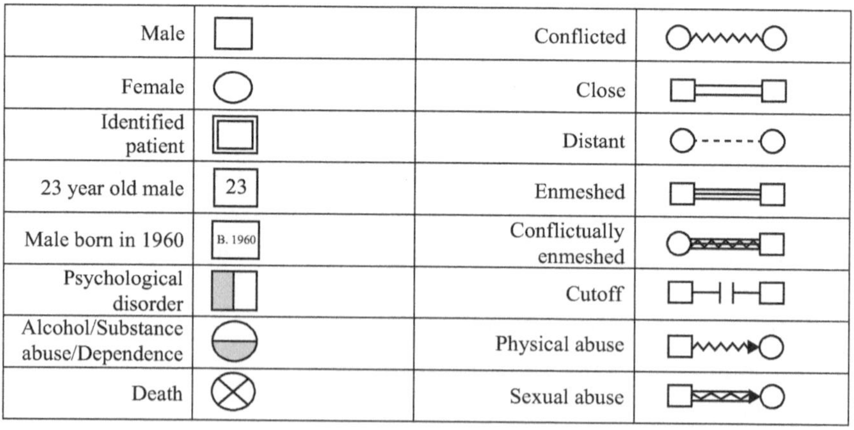

Figure 5.2: Commonly used genogram symbols

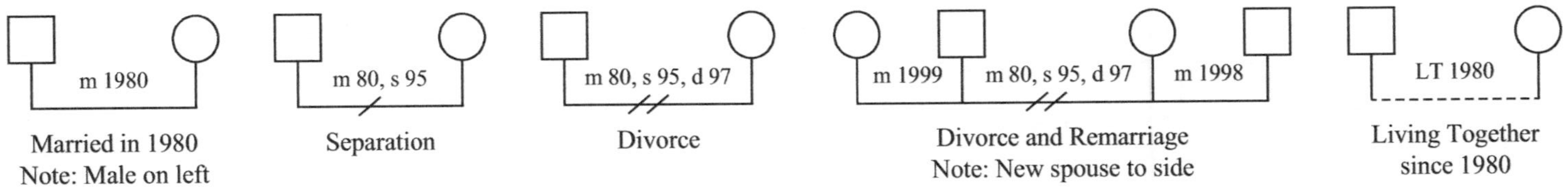

Figure 5.3: Couple relationship symbols

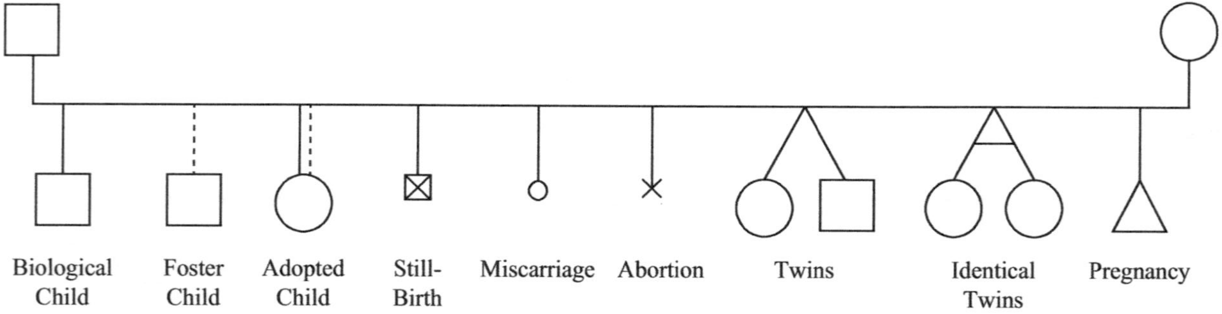

Figure 5.4: Children symbols

Building a Working Alliance with the Family

Building a strong working alliance is critical for effective therapy because without it family therapy may not be successful (Carr, 2005). These alliances are even more important when working with Muslim families given the crucial role of strong relationships in collectivistic cultures' relational patterns. Warmth, empathy, and genuineness are some of ways for therapists to develop a working alliance with family members (Sprenkle & Blow, 2004). The therapist and the family must collaborate at a level such that all family members feel comfortable providing information about the particular qualities of each individual in the family, and the therapist should provide broad scientific and clinical data that are pertinent and relevant to family development. Evaluation should be conducted with respectful curiosity to uncover new information about the problem and potential solutions. This kind of curiosity helps the family think about their difficulties from several different perspectives.

Family therapy should be conducted in a way to match clients' readiness to change so the therapeutic alliance won't get jeopardized. Muslim families living in or coming from collectivistic societies do not have much exposure to psychotherapy language and may not value insight and perception as much as Westerners. Thus, when therapists offer a set of techniques on how to change a certain behavior without clients understanding why they should change that behavior, it makes them feel pressured. Thus, they may not complete any of their homework assignments, making the therapist feel frustrated about the clients' resistance. Therapists need to offer a great deal of psychoeducational information about why family members should change their behaviors or interactional patterns.

Stage 3: Treatment

Based on the information provided by the family during the evaluation stage, the family may be encouraged to make a contract for treatment. In some instances, the process of evaluation may lead to problem resolution, and, therefore, treatment may not be needed. For example, if the therapist manages to successfully reframe the problem in a way that allows the family to gain a new perspective and see it as normal reaction, part of a developmental phase, or a temporary problem. In some other situations, the assessment process allows family members to use their instinctual problem-solving abilities and resolve their problem without needing further consultations. For example, some parents become more confident about handling their child's behavior once they discuss and process their anxiety during the first family interviews. In other situations, evaluation leads to a treatment contract. It is important for therapists to remember that treatment is rarely a predictable process and that relationship difficulties, resistances, and impasses that may develop in the mid-phase of treatment require extensive skills, especially if the therapist and the family do not share the same cultural and religious background.

Forming a Therapeutic Contract

Based on the information provided at the evaluation stage, developing a treatment contract involves creating clearly defined goals and delineating a plan to work towards those goals. It is important to have realistic and clear goals that all family members can agree on in order for therapy to be effective. It may be helpful to ask clients to envision how their daily activities will be different if the issue at hand were resolved, which in turn helps clients with articulating their therapeutic goals. It is important to have family members think about very small steps for change. Very often, once these small changes occur and family members realize the positive impact on their daily functioning, positive changes become more magnified even without more therapeutic intervention (Segal, 1991).

Therapists should be able to measure progress towards goals by utilizing behavioral frequencies, like the number of compliments family members give each other, the number of fights, the number of nights going to bed on time, or the number of times the child listens to her parents' requests. Progress in having better moods and change in beliefs can also be measured using scaling questions, such as, "If on a scale of 1–10 your mood is about 3 right now, what number may indicate that you are recovering?" Or, "If you start to feel better, what number do you think represents your mood on a 10-point scale on most days?" These are all helpful ways of giving the family a quantifiable way of thinking about their feelings and moods. These techniques are important because Muslim families are often very intertwined relationally and may have a hard time separating small progress from unachievable and grandiose relational goals.

It is challenging to work with different family members with setting common goals because they may have different priorities; thus, negotiating their goals and taking each family member's costs and benefits may become very essential. Asking questions regarding each person's gain or loss if they effectively accomplished their goal will be helpful in creating a therapeutic contract. Family therapists have to deal with the conflicting needs and wishes of each family member and need to help with the articulation of the similarities and differences between each family member's positions and goals. However, the power hierarchy in Muslim families needs to be taken into consideration because it may prevent all family members from equally accomplishing their goals. A skillful therapist must be able to work with these power hierarchies and help each family member's position be considered and valued.

Salma, a 14-year-old girl who had to see a therapist because of relational difficulties with her parents, stated that becoming more independent was her main goal but that her parents' goal was for her to be more compliant, and since they had more power in the relationship, she was feeling stuck. When Salma and her parents were asked if they had any common goals, they all said they wanted to be able to have more harmony in their relationships and get along better. Further, when both Salma and her parents were questioned about what would be different if Salma became both independent and compliant, they all wanted Salma to get a scholarship for college. They all agreed that this could help Salma accomplish her own goal of working on being a better student and satisfy her parents' goal of her compliantly getting her schoolwork done. Therefore, the therapy goal was set at getting higher grades in important subjects, which also reflected the family goal of reducing relational conflicts.

Once a comprehensive examination of different goals is done, clients should accept working on the set of goals. Therapists should make sure that the clients are accepting and committed to the therapeutic process before any discussions of ways of achieving those goals. Culturally relevant and specific research about the risks and benefits of family interventions should be shared with clients. For example, generally, in the US, most effective relational interventions for families are successful in only about 66%–75% of cases, and about 10% of cases worsen as a consequence of therapy (Carr, 2000a, 2000b; Sprenkle, 2002). Families that have lots of strengths are more likely to benefit from therapy, and most fundamental progress happens in the first 6–10 sessions. The same relevant research must be shared with Muslim families in each society so they can relate to other families' struggles and learn about what is helpful and not so helpful about psychotherapy. Setbacks and disappointment are expected with various kinds of conflicts, and intermittent meetings may become essential in helping families manage relapse situations. If there are persistent problems and conflicts, additional interventional sessions are typically offered at life cycle transitions.

Once therapy goals have been discussed and contracts have been established, treatment should be started. Treatment may involve interventions that focus on altering behaviors, can focus on helping families develop new belief systems and narratives that can create new possibilities for problem solving, or can possibly focus on contextual, historical, or other predisposing factors. It is perhaps more effective if we first start with interventions that aim to change behavioral patterns and their underlying belief systems, except when our clinical judgment reveals that the interventions will not be effective because of some historical family of origin conflicts or larger circumstantial dynamics. If these interventions that center around problem-maintaining behavior patterns and belief systems are not effective, then we should move towards interventions that target historical and contextual factors. Muslim families may respond well to these historical and contextual assessments and interventions since their behaviors are deeply embedded in their history and culture.

Management of Resistance

Family therapists often have to deal with this interesting paradox that clients go great lengths to seek professional assistance to manage their relational problems but very often do not follow through with the given therapeutic advice to resolve their presenting problems. Muslim families may not even comprehend the usefulness of the therapeutic interventions, but in Western psychology we still call their behavior resistance. Family therapists need to accept that clients' resistance is inevitable and part of any therapist–client relationship and not assume that only Muslim families may be resistant to change. Nevertheless, therapists need to develop skills to manage resistance because these skills will contribute to a very effective practice of family therapy (Nichols, 2013). In many situations, if therapists take their clients' readiness for change into account, resistance can be avoided (deShazer, 1988; Prochaska, 1999). In the early stages of therapy, the clients need to receive support and validation because family members, a school, or the court system may have coerced the family into seeking therapy.

Once clients begin the process of dealing with their problems and considering the possibility of solving them, they may be ready to examine the costs and benefits of change. Clients' uncertainty with regards to change may originate from being demoralized, overwhelmed, or afraid of change. These uncertainties will be very apparent for Muslim immigrant families living in the West who feel judged and devalued. It is the therapist's responsibility to prove to the Muslim family that their struggles are understood and their opinions are valued. Once clients pass the stage of uncertainty and doubt, they need help to brainstorm problem-solving strategies and require help and support from the therapist to create an action plan. Clients may need to have some sessions with the therapist after they have made considerable changes in order to maintain these changes. Resistance will develop in the therapeutic relationship if therapists do not match their relational interventions with clients' inclination to change. For instance, therapists may prematurely propose some ideas for problem solving to clients, but clients may still be exploring the pros and cons of change and contemplating new possibilities. Thus, clients may resist if there is too much pressure, and no therapeutic tasks will be accomplished. In this instance, therapists often assume that clients are resistant to change and feel disappointed about clients' lack of progress. This frustration jeopardizes the long-term effectiveness of therapy and the client and therapist alliance.

When therapists appropriately evaluate clients' resistance, they may uncover some important factors. In some situations unexpected events like acts of God may hamper progress. Muslim families may use the concepts of faith and belief that everything happens for a reason and both good and bad events are the 'will of God' (Al-Krenawi & Graham, 1999) and, therefore, may resist the idea of working on active problem solving. In others, the problem may be that the clients simply do not have the kinds of skills and abilities needed for change and therefore seem resistant. For example, when the therapeutic contract is not well established, resistance is usually due to not understanding what is expected of the client. Particular principles and values based on clients' personal, family, or cultural belief systems can also add to client resistance, if the clients' beliefs contradict the therapeutic tasks they supposed to accomplish. In many instances, avoiding emotional pain is an additional reason for resistance.

Transference and countertransference between client and therapist can also contribute a great deal to resistance to change. Some clients have trouble following through with the therapy process because of transferring the same relationship expectations they had as infants—either very supportive and nurturing or unsupportive and inattentive. Clients may want the therapist to be a supportive and nurturing parent who can free them from emotional pain, but they may have a hard time with being accountable for resolving their own issues. For example, a frustrated and helpless mother may want the therapist to somehow rescue her from dealing with the everyday behavior of a child with behavioral and emotional problems without looking at her own behavioral and emotional reactions towards the child. In some other instances, clients perceive the therapist as an inattentive and punishing parent and do not follow through with any suggestions the therapist offers. For example, if a father assumes that his values and authority in the family may be challenged by the therapist, he may decide not to participate in therapy. This may be the case for many traditional Muslim families with fathers assuming they should have a higher position in the family. In some cases, clients may alternate their positions from greatly needing assurance and support to rejecting all suggestions and advice. It is important for the therapist to identify and discuss treatment goals and the family's and the therapist's responsibilities towards achieving those goals. It may be applicable to discuss issues of transference by comparing the resemblance between the clients' relationships with their parents and their current relationships with the therapist. This may become a very important therapeutic task given the high level of parental involvement in the life of children in many Muslim families. However, these discussions are only suitable when there is a strong therapeutic alliance and clients are emotionally stable and can handle such conversations.

Most therapists experience some dissatisfaction or frustration when they have to deal with client reactions and resistance. However, when the therapists' negative reactions to clients who may not be cooperating with the therapeutic process seem out of proportion to the clients' actual behavior, therapists may be experiencing countertransference.

This means that therapists are reacting based on early life experiences and transferring their own relationship expectations onto their current relationships with clients. When strong countertransference reactions happen and therapists act on these feelings without supervision or personal reflection, they can no longer maintain their therapeutic neutrality and may replicate problematic family behavioral patterns. For example, a therapist's countertransference may impact the family when child neglect, abuse, or delinquency issues force the therapist to pressure the family to change their behavior, and family's resistance may result in punishing the client. It is possible, then, for the family to repeat the punishing behavior and the child neglect, abuse, or delinquency to continue.

STAGE 4: TERMINATION

The termination process begins when progress and improvement are noticed. The sessions can be scheduled with a longer interval between them. This can be helpful for clients to know that the therapist believes in their ability to cope and handle their own relational difficulties without the therapist's assistance. If goals have been achieved, the therapist aids the family in having a better understanding of the change process and reviews the initial problem formulation and clients' progress and improvements through the treatment process.

Family members are coached on how to make plans for managing setbacks and to anticipate the types of stressful situations in which setbacks can happen. They should also discuss their possible negative reactions to setbacks and ways they can deal with these setbacks with what they have learned in therapy in a productive way. There are many somewhat simple behavioral problems that can be used to introduce the idea of setbacks. Bedwetting, head banging, extreme emotional reactions, smoking, thumb sucking, and nail-biting are some examples to consider. After all family members have acknowledged that setbacks can happen, the therapist can ask questions about how family members plan to predict, respond to, and anticipate these events. The therapist can ask that if the setbacks and relapses were going to happen, in what circumstance are they most likely to occur and what signs does the family need to look for?

Often setbacks are directly related to the original problems and triggered under similar situations that caused the original problems. When setbacks occur as an anniversary reaction, it is often related to a major loss or bereavement that perhaps was the reason for the original referral. Setbacks are largely intertwined with a series of demanding life events like individuals joining or leaving the family; divorces or remarriages; school or residency changes for children; illness in family; work situation changes for parents; or financial status changes for family members. After all these setbacks have been discussed with family members, some questions may be asked about the way a setback can be prevented. The consultation process about these setbacks can be entertaining and interesting because the therapist can encourage clients to overstate and exaggerate family members' spontaneous and instinctive reactions to these setbacks and how these reactions may lead to an intensification of the problem.

In working with Muslim families, it often makes perfect sense to work with different family configurations without worrying about losing therapeutic connections with each individual. Therefore, the therapist may end one therapeutic contract and begin another one. For example, after a period of working with a family focusing on children's issues, a following contract may center around marital issues of the parents, extended family issues, or individual work with adults in the family.

There are times during the course of family therapy that the therapist is doing more of the same and treatment goals are not reached (Segal, 1991). In these instances, lack of progress in achieving therapeutic goals must be analyzed in a systematic way, which is extremely valuable for the clients and the therapist. There are many reasons for failures to occur. First, the family member who may have a direct influence on change in the family may not have been part of the family therapy process. For example, when a child has emotional or behavioral problems and fathers are not involved and engaged in the therapy process, change may be less likely. This may be especially true for Muslim families when fathers' opinions and perspectives are supposed to be greatly respected and valued. Second, the family belief system about the problem may not have fit with what the therapist believed needed to be changed. Third, the therapeutic coalition may not have been adequate, and the therapist may have had difficulties convincing family members to complete the therapeutic tasks. Fourth, families' reservations and resistance to change may not have been processed adequately. Fifth, the therapist may have disengaged without empowering the family to handle relapses.

Sixth, countertransference may have been an issue where the therapist's responses to family issues seriously compromised the therapist's neutrality and capacity to join each member of the family system in an empathic way. Finally, family limitation in achieving therapeutic goals may not have been taken into account. These limitations include: families of origin unresolved issues; problems with the wider social system, such as poverty; and issues related to vulnerability to illness or disability. It is important for family therapists to analyze treatment failure since it enhances therapeutic skills.

Summary

In working with Muslim families, family therapy has to be conceptualized as an evolving, progressing, and recursive process that includes the stages of preparation, evaluation, treatment, and termination. In the preparation stage, it is important to involve individuals significantly impacted by the problem to the initial interview. The minimum appropriate group that need to be present for an evaluation includes the person seeking help, the person who is legally responsible for the person believed to have a problem, the person who is supportive and has empathy towards the referred person, and the referred person. During the first few sessions, planning based on the therapist's conceptualization, creating a therapeutic contract, managing family engagement issues, establishing a therapeutic coalition, and offering constructive advice are some of the most important features of the evaluation stage. It is extremely important to work on establishing a working alliance and a strong connection with the family; otherwise, clients may not continue the consultation process.

The therapist's relationship with the family should be a collaborative partnership based on respectful curiosity, warmth, compassion, responsiveness, and authenticity. The therapeutic approach and the clients' readiness to change should be matched. Any issues related to clients' transference and the therapist's countertransference in the therapeutic relationship should be recognized. Undoubtedly, cooperation and collaboration difficulties will occur during the course of therapy. These may be due to complex reasons that impact clients' motivation to resolve their difficulties or lack of clients' or therapist's skills. Clients' resistance and the therapist's lack of appropriate skills in resolving the clients' resistance need to be assessed in order to complete the treatment plan. When goals on the therapeutic contract have been reached, the termination process should be considered. If goals have not been accomplished, the therapist needs to acknowledge it, and possible referral to another therapist should be considered. Where goals have been accomplished, possible future setbacks can be discussed, and the family should be given the option to come back for additional sessions. If other problems emerge, the therapist should offer a new contract to work on those issues. Overall, even though there are specific challenges and particular issues related to the cultural backgrounds of Muslim families, there are many similarities in ways we can provide family therapy cross-culturally that can go beyond specific cultural relationship patterns.

REFERENCES

Al-Krenawi, A., & Graham, R.G. (1999). Social work and Koranic mental health healers. *International Social Work, 42*, 53–65. doi:10.1177/002087289904200106

Carr, A. (2000a). Research update: Evidence based practice in family therapy and systemic consultation. I: Child focused problems. *Journal of Family Therapy, 22*, 29–59.

Carr, A. (2000b). Research update: Evidence based practice in family therapy and systemic consultation. II: Adult focused problems. *Journal of Family Therapy, 22*, 273–295.

Carr, A. (2005). Research on the therapeutic alliance in family therapy. In. C. Flaskas, B. Mason, & A. Perlesz (Eds.), *The space between experience, context and process in the therapeutic relationship* (pp. 187–199). London: Karnac.

deShazer, S. (1988). *Clues: Investigating solutions in brief therapy.* New York: Norton.

Nichols, M. (2013). *Family therapy: Concepts and methods* (10th ed.). Boston: Pearson.

Prochaska, J. (1999). How do people change and how can we change to help many more people. In M. Hubble, B. Duncan, & D. Miller (Eds.), *The heart and soul of change* (pp. 227–259). Washington, DC: APA.

Segal, L. (1991). Brief therapy: The MRI approach. In A. Gurman & D. Kniskern (Eds.), *Handbook of family therapy* (Vol. 2, pp. 17–199). New York: Brunner/Mazel.

Sprenkle, D. (2002). *Effectiveness research in marital and family therapy.* Alexandria: American Association for Marital and Family Therapy.

Sprenkle, D.H., & Blow, A.J. (2004). Common factors and our sacred models. *Journal of Marital & Family Therapy, 30*, 113–129. doi:http://dx.doi.org/10.1111/j.1752-0606.2004.tb01228.x

CHAPTER 6

STRUCTURAL FAMILY THERAPY

Salvador Minuchin, an Argentinean psychiatrist, developed a model for treatment based on systems theory called structural family therapy. Structural family therapy is unique because of its emphasis on structural change having priority over the details of individual change (Minuchin, 2014). The therapist acts as a leader and a very dynamic mediator trying to restructure the family. This treatment model works well with the Eastern family backgrounds of most Muslim families in terms of honoring expert opinions and following advice as opposed to insight-oriented therapy. Structural family therapy uses three related parts—the family as an open living system, the problem behavior, and therapeutic change—in order to alter the family dynamics.

THE FAMILY AS AN OPEN LIVING SYSTEM

The family is conceptualized as a living open system (Minuchin, 1970) that is influenced by and influences its environment. This indicates that families are the only system influencing and impacting their own way of relating, even though cultural patterns also shape family interactions. Based on this model, Mr. Ahmed's detached connection to his son Mohammed is the consequence of Mrs. Ahmed's over-involvement with Mohammed. Further, this distinct family arrangement works for them and also serves as a strong connection to their Middle Eastern cultural background that supports closeness of mothers to their children and encourages fathers to have more distance.

Further, since families are a living system, they are constantly changing and evolving as each family member negotiates the kind of particular arrangements they think are effective for their survival. This progression is structured around the interaction between homeostasis, or stability, and change. The state of homeostasis is about transactional patterns that guarantee the system's stability and the preservation of its essential characteristics. In other words, homeostatic processes tend to keep the system at a stable place. Minuchin calls this state of homeostasis that interconnects individual behaviors like the pieces in a puzzle complementarity (2014).

On the contrary, the living system undergoes a process of change to adjust to constantly changing environmental conditions or to essential developmental needs. Mohammed and his parents may need to change their interactional dynamics if they have another child. Developmental changes like births, marriage, going to school, beginning the adolescence years, going to college, or starting a new job are examples that impact the life of most families while losing a job, an unexpected death in the family, a job promotion, relocating to another city, or a divorce are distinctive events that affect the journey of some families. These changes affect family patterns and may create complexity in the family system. In the structural family therapy model, there should be subsystems like spousal subsystems, parent-child subsystems, and sibling subsystems that are supposed to co-exist together. These systems may need new rules to further define different levels of participation, inclusion, and exclusion in different situations. These subsystems and their relationships with each other are called boundaries. Mr. and Mrs. Amin will not allow children to participate in adults' arguments because they have good boundaries. The oldest son, Ali, and his father can spend time alone together and create their own healthy subsystem, and the oldest daughter, Maryam, can ask for more privacy in the house compared to her younger siblings.

It is important to note that homeostasis and change are part of family processes for all families. If we observe a family over time, we will see the homeostatic mechanisms working and keeping the system in relative equilibrium. However, sometimes a crisis happens and challenges the family's stability. These crises should be an exception in the family life, but when there are multiple crises and the family is dealing with many changes, family homeostasis becomes seriously affected. The family may not be able to respond to new environmental or developmental demands; may have a hard time utilizing new ways of interacting; and may rely on old dysfunctional but familial patterns. In the Ahmed family's situation, Mr. and Mrs. Ahmed may not be able to change the passivity/initiative arrangement even if they all realize the interaction is not working. Mohammed and his mother will continue to have the same level of closeness that was developmentally appropriate at 2 but not appropriate at 18. It is possible that Mohammed's school attendance problems started at 12 but that his family maintained the same structure since his mother was the only one monitoring all communication with school. Thus, Mohammed did have to deal with his father's anger, and his father did not have to deal with his own sense of disappointment and frustration.

Transactional patterns in families become fixed and static when families get developmentally stuck. Homeostatic mechanisms intensify even more when the family system gets trapped in the same dysfunctional relational patterns and all the changes deviating from familiar patterns are instantly modified. If Mohammed's father wants to hold him accountable, his mother will immediately interfere, and his father will immediately back off. Thus, intergenerational alliances of mother and son against father will weaken the expected mother and father natural hierarchies. Further, the triangulation patterns of each parent demanding a child to side with him or her, and other nonfunctional arrangements, prevent the onset of open conflict in the system. Thus, avoiding the conflict creates a sense of stability but prevents families from developmental progress, differentiation, and conflict resolution. According to structural family therapy, enmeshed families have higher levels of conflict avoidance, and chances of disagreements are minimized due to their extreme sense of closeness, belonging, and loyalty (Minuchin, 1970). This is a very typical pattern for Muslim families. On the other hand, disengaged families also have minimum disagreements, but their false sense of independence is produced by excessive distance.

Family members hold on to the myths of very narrow definitions of themselves as a whole in order to keep their pseudo balance and present themselves less competent than they really are: "I am who I am and act the way I do and cannot act any other way; the same is true for all my family members, and we cannot relate to each other in any other way than our way."

The Problem Behavior

Structural family therapy views behavioral problems as part of families' transactional process. Mohammed's behavioral problems are related to not being disciplined and being allowed to act aggressively, which is directly related to his family context. The therapist, then, has to search for the function of Mohammed's behavioral problems to find out: Under what circumstance did Mohammed become aggressive? What usually happens before? How does each family member respond to his behavior? Does Mohammed act more aggressively with his mother or with his father? Do his parents agree on how to handle his behavior? How does the homeostatic family system benefit from the progressive patterns of his problem behavior? In this system, Mohammed's behavioral problem complements his parents' behaviors and keeps the system at equilibrium, and this powerful and stable system supports the symptoms.

The structural therapist has also the task of diagnosing the family system's perceptions of the presenting problem. Who in the family system is more concerned about Mohammed's disruptive behavior? Who thinks he is aggressive? Who thinks his behavior is the most problematic issue in the family? Do Mohammed's positive traits go unnoticed? Is the family exaggerating and over-labeling Mohammed's 'aggressive' behavior? Is the family not recognizing Mohammed's developmental needs now that he is 18 years old? A structural therapist is able to see that the family system draws a homeostatic gain based on perceiving Mohammed as a symptomatic child.

Thus, in this model, the presenting problem is directly connected to the interactional network in the family. Thus, there is a direct connection between problem behavior and family system, and the emphasis is on how the family system maintains the problem. Undoubtedly, sometimes when therapists assess families, the connection between the transactional structure and the symptoms are very obvious. But therapists have to remember that the present transactions and memories are organized after the formation of the problem. The structural family therapy model looks for a constant progression of reciprocal accommodation between family members' predispositions and vulnerabilities and the family system's rules. Perhaps Mohammed's strong temperament challenged his family system to somehow pay closer attention to his tantrums and ignore his positive behaviors. Within this family context Mohammed learned about how he should behave and about the benefits of acting aggressively. By the time he turned eight, Mohammed was a skillful contributor to a mutually intensifying game of disobedience and punishment. These processes of paying attention to a series of behaviors and labeling it as abnormal are some of the ways family systems contribute to the etiology of a 'problem.' Mohammed's cousin Ali, who is the same age as him, had the same 'strong temperament,' but he is now the youth leader and a soccer player.

Therapeutic Change

Structural family therapy's basic principle is based on the idea that any presenting problem or dysfunction that families bring to therapy is related to the entire family structure and not just one individual. Therefore, structural therapy seeks a therapeutic solution to modify the family structure. This frequently entails modifications and alterations of the positions of family members with each other, such as a healthy detachment between mother and son and more closeness between spouses. Coalitions and relational hierarchies often need to be redefined. New rules of interactions must be discovered. Mohammed's mother, for example, should be instructed to refrain from interfering whenever her son and husband's interactions become more conflictual, and Mohammed and his father's arguments should not repeatedly end when the mother is upsets. Conflicts should be openly recognized, analyzed, and discussed in order to be resolved.

Families need to be assisted with outgrowing their fixed patterns of holding on to their presenting problem through the process of therapeutic change. This process emerges within a relational context of the therapeutic system challenging family rules and relational patterns. The hierarchical position of the structural therapist gives her permission to ask family members to exhibit different behaviors and to have different perceptions in order to change their interactions and perspectives. This new pattern of interaction gives the family an opportunity to experience the kind of relationship they have not experienced in the homeostatic state.

The family system's boundaries are explored and challenged, and its limited self-definitions are examined. As the family's tolerance to cope with stress or conflict increases, their perception of reality becomes deeper and more profound. Structural therapists use the family itself to change attitudes, perceptions, affinities, and expectations.

Therapeutic Application

Structural family therapy is a coherent way of thinking and working with families and originated from the basic principle that human problems could only be treated and understood within the boundaries of family relational context. Therefore, the structural model is appropriate for any human system that needs to undergo a fundamental change. It is important to note that families are unique because as a natural group they share a common history and a common future. For instance, Muslim family members often stay connected even when they are dealing with difficult conditions like extreme negative feelings towards each other and high levels of constant conflict.

Structural family therapy has been mostly used with families where the identified patient is a child because the family context is the most appropriate setting and the child's emotional health is the responsibility of parents (Minuchin, 1970). Structural family therapy is appropriate for families who are motivated and resourceful, and systemic thinking tells us that there are no families without resources and that any family can potentially be motivated.

Aims and Purpose of Therapy

The primary aim of structural family therapy is restructuring transactional rules in the family so family members can interact with each other more flexibly. Therefore, family reorganization and freeing family members from their inflexible positions enhances their ability to activate their own underutilized resources and cope with stress and conflict (Minuchin, 2014). Thus, therapy ends when the family reaches autonomy in maintaining the new acquired changes and does not need the challenging support of the therapist. In order to get the family to the point of self-sufficiency, the therapist's function is to assist the family in changing their ways of interacting and to not assign rigid meanings to each interaction and behavior. Furthermore, in the structural family therapy model, the therapist helps the family developmental process in the family's own natural human context so family members can provide support to each other and help each other grow. Thus, the therapist's major task is not mainly to listen to and provide answers for clients' fears, fantasies, and wishes (Minuchin, 2014).

Therapist's Role

The therapist's role in this model is paradoxical. The therapist is supposed to be supporting while challenging, attacking while encouraging, and maintaining the status quo while undermining familial but dysfunctional patterns. A structural family therapist's first task is to enter the family system, creating a functioning and operational alliance, which demands adaptation to individual and family rules in the family system. However, the therapist should be distanced enough so her influence in promoting change cannot be lost. The therapist's task is to find the right balance between accommodating and challenging each family through a process of searching for helpful clues, expanding possibilities, and retracing challenges that guide her access and give her clues about the family structure. Thus, neutral listening is not a useful skill for the structural family therapist. The structural therapist should have a series of primary assumptions based on the information provided by family during intake but should continue to assess, develop, and change preliminary assumptions as she gets to know the family over time. The main goal should be paying attention to process and not content. The therapist should be more interested in how family members relate to each other than in what they say to each other and should listen to the content of the conversation only to understand the family's use of language. Some themes and ideas may unravel as the therapist pays selective attention to some and discards others. A family interaction map may emerge, representing positions, alliances, hierarchies, and complementary patterns. Family members are invited to talk to each other so the distances and positions can be understood and some alternative arrangements can be tried. The therapist uses the knowledge gained to create situations that will help with uncovering hidden resources and finding each family member's personal limitations and challenges.

While the structural family therapy model advocates for action, creativity, and direct suggestion, it also cautions against the centrality of the therapist's position. The therapist's task is to set up a scenario and get family members to act and then simply be an observer of family interactions. If the therapist's role becomes excessively central, the family system cannot completely show its potentialities and limitations. Therefore, the therapist gets stuck in a stereotyped position and will most likely be immersed into family homeostasis. The therapist has to be active and continuously change positions. She needs to shift roles, change alliances, challenge family interactional patterns, and maintain a focus in order to connect all the family interactions together and to the presenting problem. Therefore, the therapist has to be active in blocking rigid and static relational patterns of connections and communication and promoting the development of more flexible ones.

JOINING TECHNIQUES

The family and the therapist go through a joining process that often leads to the development of a functional therapeutic system. During the process of joining, the family hopefully accepts the therapist, and if the joining process is successful, the therapist keeps the position as the therapy progresses. Even though the joining process at the beginning phase of therapy is more obvious, it is the therapist's job to maintain this working relationship with the family. If the therapist is able to listen, empathize, be genuinely interested in the family's dramas, and remain sensitive to feedback, the joining process will be successful. However, the therapist needs some techniques for joining the family. The therapist needs to carefully control her level of empathy so that it does not inhibit her ability to keep a healthy therapeutic distance from the family and work towards the course of change. It is a mistake to assume that joining means being accepted to provide therapy. It is about being accepted as a therapist and being able to lead and guide the family and push for change and not being swallowed by the homeostatic rules of the system.

One of the major techniques of joining is maintenance, which means that the therapist relies on the fundamental rules and regulations that synchronize the transactional process in the family system to alter family interactions. If, for example, a four-generation family presents a rigid hierarchical structure, which may be very typical in Eastern and Muslim families, the therapist may make a connection to the great-grandmother or great-grandfather first and then progress to the next generation. In this way, the therapist will still show empathy to the identified patient but by honoring the family's systems she will have a much better chance to have a therapeutic impact on the entire family.

However, in order to prevent total submission and acceptance of family rules, the therapist needs to behave in a way that does not leave her powerless. It is important to note that like any other joining technique, maintenance also requires challenging the system. For example, the therapist can talk to the grandmother with respect but also say: "I am very concerned because I see all of you struggling to help, but you are not being helpful to each other." In this way, the family rule of 'grandma's opinion first' is honored at one level at the same time that the therapist is putting herself on the top of the hierarchy in relation to the whole system, including the grandmother.

Whereas maintenance focuses on family process, the tracking technique comprises the adaptation of the therapist to the content of the conversation in which the therapist follows the conversation carried on by family members. This allows her to join the family culture and also become familiar with unique metaphors and jargons the family uses. The therapist can later use these metaphors the family uses with additional power. In some situations, the therapist needs to establish a closer relation with one specific family member who has been positioned by the family on the outside of the system.

Changing Family Dynamics Techniques

The second, larger group of techniques covers all interventions that intend to change the family system. Some like enactment and boundary making are mainly used to create a special order of events. Some other techniques like reframing, punctuating, and unbalancing promote a different way of perceiving reality in families.

Reframing

Reframing is an effective technique for viewing the presenting problem from a different perspective. Normally this includes shifting the meaning and definition of the original complaint based on how the therapist understands the core of the presenting problems in families. In this situation, she needs to be keenly looking for structural patterns so she can use them in her communications with the family. After the presenting problem is reframed and defined as, for example, complementarity, family members' participation in the therapeutic work would create a different meaning for them. So when family members' interactions are labeled as reciprocally causing more problems, the key to resolving the problem has been given to them. It is important to note that complementary relationships are not essentially negative. Complementarity is indeed part of everyday life experiences, and it can be used to help family members change. Within this framework, the therapist can ask the family members to enact an alternate interaction.

Enactment

Based on the structural family therapy model, enactment shows all transactional patterns the therapist can control and use to help families change. This technique helps the therapist understand the mutual behavioral regulations in families and also locate where the problem behavior mostly occurs once she observes the sequences of family interactions (Minuchin, 1970). Enactment is also the tool the therapist uses to disrupt the existing patterns, examining how the family system is able to adjust itself to different circumstances and eventually making the experimental and alternate scenario, the new and more functional rules. Change is anticipated to transpire because the family is dealing with the problems, instead of talking about them. Enactment is supposed to provide an alternative way for families to perceive their own reality. Any justifications family members have for their behaviors; their viewpoints, functions, and contributions to the solution for the problems in the family; and their reciprocal positions in the family are typically examined by these transactional experiences organized by the structural therapist.

Enactments can be powerful and intense or can be discreetly thrown into the conversation by the therapist with a simple, "Talk to your son about your concerns, I don't know that he understands your position" (Rosman, Minuchin, & Liebman, 1977, pp. 166–169). If this request is, for example, directed at the father who usually talks to his son by talking to his wife, and if the therapist challenges the mother to stay out of this interaction, the structural change affecting the family's behavior and perceptions would be powerful, even if the conversation that follows wouldn't be interesting. The actual power of enactment is not about creating an emotionally charged interaction. It is more about how family members are encouraged to conduct themselves differently towards each other. The therapist assumes control over the family's transactional change by prescribing and monitoring specific interactions. She basically regulates the interactional patterns of how family members interact, what the topics of their discussions are, when they talk to each other, and how long they need to discuss the same topic.

Boundary Making

Boundary making is related to enactment because the therapist helps the family change their interactional patterns. When Minuchin, for example, prevents the husband from "helping" his wife control their daughter's behavior, he is signifying that these specific transactions are between the mother and daughters to discuss and negotiate and that the father should not be part of the interaction. Minuchin calls this explicit method of boundary making "blocking" (Minuchin, 2014). There are other examples of boundary making including physically moving a family member to sit somewhere else, such as asking a child to move from in between her parents and sit on a chair away from them so she is no longer 'caught in the middle.'

Boundary making is a restructuring technique and intervention because it changes the interactional patterns and interrupts detouring mechanisms and other conflict-avoidance patterns. The father of the 10-year-old is put in charge of firmly redirecting his son's behavior without his wife's help, husband and wife solve a problem when their daughter can refrain from being the buffer, father and son talk to each other without the mother intervening—all are examples of using boundary making techniques.

Punctuations

There are many powerful events that can be noticed by the therapist in a particular session, but the lasting change in the family dynamic is mainly contingent upon the therapist's punctuation of these events. It seems like punctuation impacts family interaction in many ways. Structural therapists know that different family members can describe transactional event in different terms because their viewpoints and emotional attachments are at a different level. In a typical Muslim family, the husband may say that he needs to go to his parents' house because he cannot handle his wife's constant complaining, and she may say that his loyalty to his mother instead of her is the main source of her complaints. These conversations show the same pattern of interaction, but when the husband and wife are describing the same situation, they may begin and finish their sentences with different emphases at different points of the conversation. The structural therapist will use this information to create therapeutic change by punctuating the selective depiction of a transaction in harmony with the therapist's goals. Using the punctuation technique with this scenario, the therapist can ask the wife to discuss how her husband's lack of attention to her contributes to her complaining, instead of talking about his loyalty to his mother.

Intensity is another punctuation technique and includes underscoring the importance of an event hoping to gain the family's attention and energy on an important transactional issue. Usually the therapist makes a big deal out of something the family didn't pay close attention to or has taken for granted to challenge the reality of the interactional family system. Intensity can sometimes be accomplished through repeating the same question over and over again or through emotionally charged interventions or confrontation. It is instrumental for the structural family therapist to assess the level of the therapeutic process's intensity so that the family system's distress level is not too intolerable or too comfortable.

Unbalancing

Structural family therapists rely on unbalancing as a therapeutic intervention in supporting one member of the family in conflict with another member, thus interfering with the homeostasis of the family system. Even though unbalancing is undeniably and inevitably unfair, it is not arbitrary, and the therapist relies on particular skills to enhance the family's ability to interconnect after helping them get rid of some dysfunctional and static family dynamics. The following case example may help to apply some of these important therapeutic concepts and make sense of their usefulness in working with Muslim families.

Case Example

The Monsef family was referred to me by another therapist in my office who briefly provided therapy to the youngest son, Majid, due to his behavioral problems at home. The family included the father (Ahmed), who was 38 years old; mother (Samira), 35; Maryam, 10; and Majid, 8. The reason for the referral was that Majid was very aggressive, did not follow directions, and screamed for no apparent reason. Majid's teacher also reported some aggressive behavior at school. Mrs. Monsef's mother (Ms. Fatemeh), 64, lived with the Monsef family. Mrs. Monsef thought Majid was hyperactive and aggressive, didn't think her husband and her mother were helpful, and wanted to get help for him. Mr. Monsef worked at a factory, and Mrs. Monsef worked at a daycare. They were originally from Iran and were sponsored by Mrs. Monsef's brother to move to the US. When the family (including grandmother) came for therapy, I noticed that every time I asked the children a question, the grandmother either offered some more information or corrected the children's information. I noticed these transactions and tried to explore the family structure and reframe the problem.

After some conversations and questioning, it became apparent that Mr. Monsef was not part of the family interactions very often because Mrs. Monsef and the grandmother thought he was more tolerant of Majid's bad behavior and often allowed him to continue misbehaving or stayed calm when Mrs. Monsef and Ms. Fatemeh continued to worry about his inappropriate behavior. On the other hand, they both claimed that Mr. Monsef had bad temper and that they didn't want him to discipline Majid. I told the family that Mrs. Monsef and the grandmother had created a nice arrangement. They took care of Mr. Monsef's patience, and he only intervened when it was really necessary. However, when Majid wanted his father's attention, sometimes he had to get tougher and louder so he could get his father to interact with him instead of his mother or grandmother.

After several sessions, I was able to assess the extent of the grandmother's participation in the life of the Monsefs but did not yet challenge the grandmother's interferences. I was very much accepting of the way this family was communicating with each other but also tried to reframe the problem from a complaint about Majid's behavior into a situation that could involve all family members' interactions. I initiated challenging the family's arrangement using enactment, wanting the parents to ask Maryam to talk with the grown-ups and leave Majid playing because I believed that this would trigger Majid to act out, at which point the family transactions could be observed. As expected, Majid protested when he noticed that his sister had been invited to talk to the adults, so I asked the mother to protect Mr. Monsef's patience by intervening before things got more escalated. Mrs. Monsef tried to talk to Majid to convince him to continue playing by himself. After only a few minutes, the grandmother interrupted Mrs. Monsef and started talking to Majid, so I asked Mr. Monsef to help with the situation, but he stated that his wife and her mother took over as soon as a situation arose without asking for his input, so I asked him to discuss his viewpoints with his wife. Mr. and Mrs. Monsef had a discussion about Majid's behavior and their appropriate reactions when he refuses to respond to their demands. Mr. Monsef was supporting a more firm position, and Mrs. Monsef was supporting a more sympathetic position, while the grandmother was redirecting Majid back to playing with toys. I tried to explain to the family that the reason Majid did not follow their directives was because the grandmother was protecting Majid at all times. She was emotionally and physically available. I then invited the grandmother to come sit next to me and observe the family and not intervene. In this way, the grandmother could remain helpful, but the boundaries between her and the family were being changed.

I was also trying to punctuate the relationship between the grandmother and the family by highlighting how helpful the grandmother was in this family. This transactional pattern might have otherwise been described as the Monsefs assisting the grandmother to feel needed and helpful, or as Mrs. Monsef balancing her husband's and mother's demands by being in the middle, or as the two women having a powerful alliance against Mr. Monsef. It is clear that all these assumptions about this family's transactional and relational reality patterns were true, held the same power, and needed to be highlighted during future sessions. However, since the grandmother had a great amount of power, I did not want to create a situation to threaten the grandmother's position in the family at this time.

Over time, some sessions examined Maryam's and Majid's personality traits and their relationship with adults in the family where the children were the focus of attention. At one session, I asked Mr. Monsef to discuss some issues with the children directly in order to unbalance the family interactions and then asked the grandmother to share her observations with the family.

The Monsefs had a total of 12 weekly sessions with the entire family present. During the earlier sessions, the father and mother ineffectively argued about their son's behavior while Majid sat close to his grandmother. The first therapeutic intervention was to encourage Mr. Monsef and Majid to have an uninterrupted relationship and establish their own relational rules, without mother or grandmother interferences. This goal seemed unattainable because of this family myth that the father was somehow unable to have a relationship with his son, either because of his hot temper or his apathy. Therefore, I needed to unbalance this homeostatic situation by encouraging the father to fulfill his obligations in having a meaningful relationship with his son, challenging the mother's strong belief, and keeping the grandmother as an observer.

When Mr. Monsef became more assertive, he challenged the family system even more. He discussed his desire to go to different places with Majid alone and successfully refuted his wife's objections. The complaints about Majid's behavioral problems increasingly disappeared, and understandably the grandmother lost interest and even missed some sessions. I then decided to briefly shift my attention to the couple's relationship and work with them instead of working with the whole family.

Mrs. Monsef's father had died a few years earlier, and since Mrs. Monsef and her brother both lived in the US, and she was very close to her children, she decided to move to the US as well. When she came to the US, she lived with her son and daughter-in-law but had lots of conflicts with her daughter-in-law and eventually moved in with her daughter and concentrated her life mostly on the Monsefs. Mrs. Monsef and her mother very often talked together about the children, her husband, and probably her brother and his wife. The grandmother was also the family's baby-sitter. With the father becoming more assertive about his role in the family, the alliance between the mother and the grandmother changed, with the mother becoming more connected to her husband and more distanced from her mother. The grandmother started feeling unhappy and withdrew from interacting the same way with the children, which created problems in the mother-daughter relationship. The grandmother had been the wise and experienced one, with her role being very much respected, while Mrs. Monsef was the ineffective and anxious mother, but now Mrs. Monsef was the content and powerful family woman and the grandmother was the one assuming she was losing her powerful status in the family. At one of our family sessions, Ms. Fatemeh requested a couple of individual sessions for herself. These sessions were used for reinforcing the message of the need for her to be a loving grandmother instead of a disciplinarian undermining her daughter and her son-in-law's effort to raise their children. She processed some of her own relationship difficulties with her in-laws when she was young and felt that her children didn't respect her opinion as much as she had to respect her in-laws' and her own family's opinions about child-rearing and marital conflicts. Some of these intergenerational patterns were processed, and she agreed to rely more on her recent knowledge about family interactional patterns instead of her own painful experiences from the past.

The last sessions with the whole family were dedicated to examining the family relational changes and having new interactional rules. At that point Majid did not have any behavioral problems that the parents could not handle, and he was doing well in school. The parents had started a conversation about buying a home, an issue that had always created lots of conflict in the past because Ms. Monsef was afraid of making her husband feel incompetent and Mr. Monsef was afraid of disappointing his wife. However, based on the structural changes in the relationship, a solution-oriented conversation became more likely. And lastly, Mrs. Monsef helped her mother initiate a better and less intrusive relationship with her son and her daughter-in-law because now Ms. Fatemeh had a better understanding of her children's relationships with their spouses. She was also realizing that she could be an important part of her children' families and could gain more respect by not being directly involved with disciplining or protecting the children and by not trying to solve her adult children's relationship difficulties.

Summary

Structural family therapy is a powerful treatment model predominantly described as focusing on rudimentary and fundamental family structural changes and viewing the therapist as a dynamic and preemptive agent for a family's interactional change. This is an effective model of treatment for psychological disorders and can be successfully used to treat many emotional and relational issues in Muslim families that have intertwined and enmeshed family dynamics.

Family is an open system with interdependent individuals, and their relationships are synchronized based on the constant interaction between homeostasis and change. When families get stuck in their own interactional patterns, and cannot adjust to changing developmental and environmental strains, homeostasis becomes dominant. These families then can be described based on their intergenerational alliances, triangulations, avoidance of conflict, and lack of growth and differentiation.

In this model, the behavioral problems are perceived as only one aspect of the family stagnation. Therefore, the diagnostic assessment includes evaluating the interactional structures that are supporting rather than creating the symptom. Consequently, change in family interactions depends on how the family structure adjusts to changes in family position, increases and decreases in detachments, hierarchical relationship's redefinitions, roles and rules reevaluations, and solving conflicts; are all necessary for the family's growth and change. In this therapeutic process, the therapist encourages and pushes the family system to search for possible strengths and underutilized resources.

The structural family therapist assists the family to restructure family interaction by teaching them about clear boundaries. The therapist's role can be difficult because she has to find the right balance between accommodating and challenging the family at different points. Structural family therapy utilizes techniques to form a therapeutic system to create disequilibrium and change. Structural family therapy can be an extremely useful model in working with Muslim families due to its emphasis on issues critical to the health of Eastern families struggling with issues of boundaries and who need to work with a therapist who can be a stage director as opposed to a passive listener.

REFERENCES

Minuchin, S. (1970). *The use of an ecological framework in the treatment of a child. International yearbook of child psychiatry* (Vol. 1). New York: Wiley.

Minuchin, S. (2014). *The craft of family therapy*. New York: Routledge Press.

Philadelphia Child Guidance Clinic (Producer). (1980). *Salvador Minuchin: Taming monsters* [videotape].

Rosman, B.L., Minuchin, S., & Liebman, R. (1977). Treating anorexia by the family lunch session. In C.E. Schaefer & H.L. Millman (Eds.), *Therapies for children: A handbook of effective treatments for problem behavior* (pp. 133–154). San Francisco: Jossey Bass.

CHAPTER 7

BOWENIAN FAMILY THERAPY

Murray Bowen's family systems theory comprehensively evaluates family systems functioning (Bowen, 1966, 1978, Kerr & Bowen, 1988). Bowen's theory emphasis was on family patterns that families use to soothe and calm anxiety. Bowen believed that either extreme closeness or extreme distance generate anxiety impacting the family relationship. The family's level of anxiety is often measured by their reaction to the outside stressors and their sensitivities to specific issues passed down intergenerationally. Family members have to be able to think through their reactions to relationship problems, and if they react anxiously to these perceived emotional problems, the result will be a state of chronic anxiety and reactivity. Family therapy should attempt to lower chronic anxiety by helping family members become aware of the emotional systems and should increase the level of differentiation to emphasize self-transformation instead of changing others. This is an important model to use in working with Muslim families due to their intertwined and extremely interconnected family dynamics and because the degree of anxiety and family level of differentiation can be evaluated and appropriate interventions can be used.

BOWEN MAIN CONCEPTS

Eight interlocking concepts make up Bowen's theory. These eight concepts attempt to connect the theory to the growth and advancement of society and are not directly related to the practice of Bowenian therapy.

However, Wylie (1991) indicates that Bowen's interest in the evolutionary process and societal growth clearly differentiates him from other founders of family therapy models. As a scientist, Bowen had an ambitious goal to develop a comprehensive theory that could explain all aspects of human behavior and its roots. These eight concepts are: emotional fusion and differentiation of self; triangles; nuclear family emotional system (relational conflicts, a child or a spouse symptomatic behavior); family projection process; emotional cutoff; multigenerational transmission process; sibling positions; and societal regression (Kerr & Bowen, 1988).

Emotional Fusion and Differentiation of Self

Emotional fusion or lack of differentiation happens when having harmony within the family system is more important than honoring individual choices, which is a very typical pattern in Muslims families. Lack of differentiation is either feeling responsible for family members' reactions towards self and becoming emotionally entangled with the family or emotional cutoff from the emotional pressure in relationships (Brown, 1991; Kerr & Bowen, 1988). Bowen's clinical work with families helped him realize that it is very common for families to have changing degrees of fusion. On the other hand, differentiation is an individual's ability to function independently by personal choices while continuing to be emotionally connected to the intensity of significant relationships in a family system (Kerr & Bowen, 1988). It is important to make a distinction between Bowen's concept of fusion and what Minuchin calls enmeshment, which is lack of boundary between subsystems (Minuchin, 1974). Fusion explains an individual's reactions in a relationship as opposed to the overall structure of family relationships. Therefore, when significant family relationships are anxiously cut off, it is a sign of fusion and also intense submissiveness. When family members are in a fused relationship, they respond immediately to another family member's perceived demands, without thinking about the relational choices they may have or even discussing the relationship problems openly with the other family member. All their emotional energy is devoted to taking things personally and somehow protecting others emotionally or separating oneself to protect one's own emotions. Families that have higher inclination for emotional fusion are less flexible in their adaptation to distress, which is a typical pattern for many Muslim families.

Bowen developed a scale called differentiation of self scale in order to assess level of stress, even though it does not have a psychometric property, and it is not an actual instrument (Kerr & Bowen, 1988). Bowen stated that assessing each family member's level of differentiation depends on many factors like the person's stress level, each person's way of reacting to different stressors, and the frequency of an individual's interactions with extended family members. Bowen believed that a hypothetical complete differentiation could exist for an individual who has been able to resolve her emotional attachment to her family and can easily function without emotional fusion within her family system. This, of course, is a lifelong process, and we cannot attain total differentiation at all times. In Muslim families, the extremely intertwined relational dynamics are responsible for many family and extended family issues, and teaching family members how to differentiate from each other while keeping their connections can be extremely helpful and can change many dysfunctional interactional patterns.

Triangles

According to Bowen, triangles are the smallest and most stable relationship unit, and understanding the triangulation process is crucial in understanding Bowen's theory (Kerr & Bowen, 1988). It often happens when two people are dealing with an inevitably high level of anxiety and need to involve a vulnerable third party to relieve their anxiety. The third party either takes one person's side in the relationship or somehow serves to deter the tension and relieve the system's anxiety (Guerin, Fogarty, Fay, & Kautto, 1996; James, 1989; Lerner, 1988). For instance, when Omar begins feeling uncomfortable with too much closeness to his wife, Salma, which he sees as a sign of weakness for a man, he may begin retreating to another activity like work or go to his mother's house (the third party in the triangle). Salma then pursues Omar, which makes him withdraw even more and either work more or spend more time with his mother. Salma then feels ignored and finds assistance from a friend or family member who understands her sense of rejection. This in turn leads to Omar feeling like an outsider, so he moves anxiously closer to Salma. Under extreme stress, the triangulation process becomes more severe, and interlocking triangles get created through the whole family system. This triangulation can easily entangle the extended family or community. We have seen this happen in Muslim families when individuals find supporters to protect them or adversaries to fight against them, such as their own parents, siblings, doctors, teachers, or therapists.

According to Bowen, when everything is calm, we can hardly find triangles, but under stress, they always impact families' interactional patterns. Triangles and differentiation are closely interconnected because when there is a high level of fusion, the pull to preserve emotional stability is more intensified and a triangle is formed. The process of triangulation is not essentially dysfunctional, but the concept captures the idea that when there is anxiety in the system, the initial tension gets the system to act out elsewhere. When a third party's involvement sidetracks a dyad from solving its own relationship issues, triangulation becomes problematic, and the attention shifts to stressing out about the third party, which, in turn, prevents the dyad from solving the conflict. Triangles, according to Bowen, are often repeated across several generations. As soon as the triangled member of a relationship leaves or passes away, another family member may replace that person and play the same role. For example, a daughter may play the role of a peacemaker after her mother dies and is no longer able to mediate the tension between her husband and her son. This continuous triangle diverts and reduces the level of anxiety between fathers and sons in the family over generations. This is a very typical interactional pattern among Muslim family members where, in many instances, due to the patriarchal nature of the husband-and-wife relationship, the mother-son relationship becomes stronger than the husband-wife relationship and the mother must always mediate the relationship between her husband and son.

Nuclear Family Emotional System

Bowen emphasizes that undifferentiation has a strong impact on the emotional functioning of every family generation when we position each individual within the nuclear family emotional system. He stresses that fusion in any relationship creates triangling, which then produces symptoms in three different categories: there may be conflict in a couple's relationship, one spouse may develop some form of illness, or the problems may get projected to one or more children.

Couple Conflict

A relationship usually starts with a dyad having the same degree of desire for validation in their mutual relationship. However, one of the most important contracts in an intimate relationship is permission to disagree (Kerr & Bowen, 1988). In an undifferentiated relationship, spouses feel responsible for their partner's emotional state, and any disagreement is viewed as a personal insult and disrespect. The classic pattern in these relationships with a high level of emotional intensity is a cycle of closeness, which is often followed by conflict that creates distance, and then the couple makes up only for another cycle of intense closeness to follow. This anxiety pattern, which is called a "conflictual cocoon" (Kerr & Bowen, 1988: 192), only impacts the couples' conflict cycle and does not impact or involve children. There are three ways that couple conflict may be useful for an undifferentiated relationship, when each person believes it is possible to become more whole through the other person: 1) conflict is providing a sense of strong emotional connection with an important person; 2) conflict is justifying the maintenance of a distance in couples' relationship that is comfortable without feeling guilty about it; 3) conflict gives one person in the relationship permission to project his/her anxieties onto the partner in order to maintain a positive view of his/her own sense of self (Kerr & Bowen, 1988).

Symptoms in a Spouse

In an undifferentiated relationship, each spouse wants to relate to and fit with relational qualities of the other. Therefore, a pattern of mutual reciprocity can develop, pushing each spouse's role to opposite extremes. This fusion is described by Bowen as "the reciprocal side of each spouse's transference" (Kerr & Bowen, 1988: 170). For example, a Muslim man who is socialized to be overly responsible wants to be in a relationship with a submissive woman who is not working and relies on him for everything. However, over time, it becomes a relationship between a controlling man and a helpless wife who has given up any sense of contribution to the relationship. Both are at the same level of differentiation because their definitions of themselves are based on the other person's reactions. However, since the wife tries to adjust the most to preserve harmony in the relationship, she becomes more likely to develop emotional symptoms. Furthermore, as an under-functioning person, she gets polarized and becomes more susceptible to develop symptoms of helplessness such as depression or psychosomatic symptoms like chronic pain, which is a very common relationship pattern for Muslim couples. It is possible for the husband who is over-functioning to develop symptoms because he also becomes overwhelmed by efforts to make things right for others family members.

Family Projection Process

A child developing emotional or behavioral problems is the third symptom of lack of differentiation in a family. In the first two categories, only the couple's relationship is impacted by relational anxiety, and the children's level of functioning is not drastically influenced. However, in the family projection process, children also develop some symptoms as they become entangled in their parents' generation's relational anxiety. Typically, the child with the closest relationship with the parents and with the least amount of emotional separation is the most vulnerable to develop emotional symptoms. This often happens when there is a high level of tension in the parents' relationship, the child shows a high level of anxiety, and her emotional or behavioral reactions are wrongly viewed as the child having problems. Therefore, a detouring triangle becomes activated, and parents' attentions are transferred to the child who becomes either more demanding or impaired. For example, Sarah's school refusal distracts her mother from the quest for closeness in her relationship with her husband. Therefore, Sarah's mother's marital issues don't get resolved because the parents are invested in handling Sarah's anxiety, which may in turn make her anxiety more chronic.

Like all of Bowen's concepts, "intergenerational projection" occurs in all families to a certain degree. It may be more intense for Muslim families due to the expectation of closeness of all family members at all times. Intergenerational dynamics may influence which child may develop symptoms and at what stage of the life cycle. Family crises and their timing can also influence the susceptibility of some children to develop symptoms. According to Bowen, traumatic events underscore and highlight the family relational processes instead of actually function as the cause of family stress.

Emotional Cutoff

Emotional cutoff is the most helpful way for family members to relieve themselves from the intensity of fusion among generations. An emotional cutoff can either be reached by physical distance or using any methods of emotional retraction. Bowen makes a clear distinction between "breaking away" and "growing away" from the family. "Growing away" is considered one aspect of healthy differentiation. This means that adults keep self-determining and independent goals while continuing to see themselves are part of their family system. A 'cutoff' is used as a form of escape when family members 'decide' to be absolutely different from others in their family of origin. The cutoff may help alleviate immediate pressure, but the same patterns of reactivity in intense relationships do not change, and some forms of the same relational dynamics are repeated. These are important concepts to explore with Muslim families because of the way relationships are defined and valued in Eastern cultures and how adult children are constantly renegotiating the intensity of their closeness with their own parental system.

Bowen proposes: "If one does not see himself as part of the system, his only options are either to get others to change or to withdraw. If one sees himself as part of the system, he has a new option: to stay in contact with others and change self" (Kerr & Bowen, 1988, pp. 272–273).

It is important to remember that 'cutoffs' are not always very intense separations. For example, a hidden emotional cutoff is when Amir maintains an anxious silence in the face of his father's anger. A main assumption of this theory is the importance of maintaining emotional contact with the previous generation, which in turn helps with less emotional reactivity in the present relationships. This assumption is very important in working with Muslim families since maintaining contact with the previous generation is expected and is the healthy part of the extended family interaction. On the other hand, in the case of an emotional cutoff, the current family may experience intense emotional pressure because dealing with the unresolved conflicts from the emotional cutoff is avoided. In this situation, triangulation is a detour that family members can use to recruit supports of others and to deal with the emotional cutoff.

Multigenerational Transmission Process

Multigenerational transmission process explains how familial patterns, relational themes, family roles, and individuals' positions in triangles are transmitted intergenerationally from parents to children through the projection process. This process of multigenerational transmission varies for children based on the level of parent-child triangulation they have experienced. This model's evaluation of the presenting symptoms focuses minimally on three generations in a family. Thus, a Bowenian therapist considers analyzing family patterns over an extended period of time as forms of evaluation and intervention tools. This will help individuals in the family distance themselves from their present struggle with symptoms and find ways to change their contribution to the transmission of anxiety over the next generations.

Sibling Positions

The roles individuals tend to take in their family can be understood clearly by the sibling positioning of their family of origin. For example, the oldest child may take on more responsibility and see the need for having leadership skills, and the youngest child may become more comfortable with being dependent. Middle children typically can be more flexible in shifting between being responsible and dependent, and 'only' children are often responsible and are most likely more comfortable with the adult world. The same pattern is even more apparent for Muslim families based on many traditional values related to age and sibling positions. Bowen was interested in sibling position because he wanted to examine who in the family was the most vulnerable to being triangulated with parents. Bowen believed that a parent's identification with a child who has the same sibling position may create the same intergenerational triangles and the same relational patterns may be repeated. For example, when there is illness or death in the previous generation, the child with the same sibling position is more at risk and consequently influences the parental relationship in detouring relational tensions.

Family of origin work helps people understand their sibling positions and roles in their families. This important therapeutic process aids individuals in understanding how their sibling role experiences are determined by their family relationship expectations. It is important to note that a family's cultural and ethnic background influences the value placed on birth order position and gender. For instance, the gender of the child tends to influence the role of that child either as primarily relational (female) or primarily task oriented (male). In Muslim families, the role of the eldest son is very central in terms of taking financial responsibility for parents, and the role of the eldest daughter is crucial in terms of resolving relational issues in the family.

Societal Regression

Societal regression is a gradual ineffectiveness of functioning at societal levels, shown by, among other things, leaders' increasingly emotionally driven decisions that are inadequately supported by relevant and reasonable facts. It can be explained using the concept of emotional process in society as a reaction to persistent chronic anxiety, which is defined as responses to 'imaginary' threats that may or may not happen, in contrast to acute anxiety, which is defined as response to a 'real' threat that will almost certainly happen.

In essence, 'societal progression' is a process that occurs when humans have been able to identify more clearly and factually what issues or problems need to be addressed, in contrast to making anxiety-driven decisions about less relevant issues. During periods of progression, the sciences often flourish, and the bases for decision-making are often supported by relevant, demonstrable facts coming from advances in scientific knowledge. Many Muslim states are dealing with leaders that are part of a corrupt government system. Many others are dealing with war, ethnic tensions, and disastrous economic policies that are impacting everyday functioning of people. Therefore, family therapy should take sociopolitical conditions into consideration when working with Muslim families dealing with these issues impacting their everyday relational functioning.

Clinical Practice

Bowen was troubled by how family therapy became more technique focused (Kerr & Bowen, 1988). According to Bowen, therapy should help family members develop greater levels of differentiation so they come to blame each other less and have less emotional reactivity towards each other and take more responsibility for self within the family emotional system. Bowen's therapy is extremely unique in its focus on the importance of family of origin work of the therapists and their crucial role to direct discussion towards adults' differentiation, perceiving it as more important and central than working with children.

Bowenian family therapy has three stages: First, therapy should reduce clients' anxiety about the symptom by helping clients realize that their pattern of relating produces the emotional symptom. Second, therapy should focus on adult clients' sense of 'self' to help them work on increasing their levels of differentiation. In this process, individuals are assisted to fight against what Bowen called the "togetherness force" (Bowen, 1971 in Bowen, 1978, p. 218). Third, therapy should train adult clients to differentiate themselves from their family of origin because a higher level of differentiation decreases anxiety and increases self-responsibility when individuals interact with their nuclear family system.

Therapist Role

A Bowenian therapist connects and joins the family system but remains emotionally nonreactive. She should be able to maintain a "differentiated" position and not get stuck into an over-responsible/under-responsible position attempting to change the system. She has to be calm, attentive, and able to help the family learn about their interactional patterns in terms of being part of an emotional system. Bowen trains therapists to not see themselves as healers or helpers, so families do not wait passively to be cured. He wants therapists to try "to get the family into position to accept responsibility for its own change" (Bowen, 1971 in Bowen, 1978, p. 246). He suggests that therapists should pay close attention to their part in understanding family interactions. They should be careful they do not become a mediator getting entangled in a triangle with the family. Therefore, it is important for Bowenian therapists to understand and make significant changes in their own family of origin and increase their own level of differentiation.

Bowen put very little emphasis on learning therapeutic techniques. The therapist is only in charge of directing the therapeutic process. The process does not use enactments to block the intensification of clients' anxiety. Instead, clients should discuss their issues with the therapist in front of their family so they "listen and 'really hear' without reacting emotionally, for the first time in their lives together" (Bowen, 1971 in Bowen, 1978, p. 248). Bowenian therapists do not facilitate a conversation between the couple and interview one spouse in front of the other without asking for any emotional responses. Bowen believed that emotional responses do not lead to differentiation of self and preferred asking clients to share their "thoughts," "reactions," and "impressions," calling it "externalizing the thinking of each client in the presence of the other" (Bowen, 1971, in Bowen, 1978, p. 226).

Children

Bowen often did not involve children other than at the first few therapy sessions. He would then dismiss them to concentrate on the adults' relationship because he believed adults' interactions influence family members' relational patterns (Bowen, 1975 in Bowen, 1978, p. 298). This may be a difficult task to accomplish with Muslim families who prefer to concentrate on children's symptomology and not their own relationships. It is important to note that not allowing the child to take responsibility for therapeutic change is called a detriangulation maneuver. In this way, parents cannot triangulate the child to relieve themselves from their relational difficulties, and since the therapist also refuses to take a role in their emotional triangle, parents begin to differentiate themselves from one another.

Family Therapy

The first few sessions in Bowenian therapy are used for gathering pertinent information in order to develop some hypothesis about the emotional processes in the family and their presenting problem from a systemic perspective. The therapist pays close attention to how the presenting problem has impacted the nuclear family and continues to explore the extended family system. The information can be recorded using a multigenerational family genogram (Kerr & Bowen, 1988). The therapist explores the family's emotional process, looking for repeated patterns of regulating closeness and distance; the way family members have dealt with anxiety in the system; activated triangles; the family's level of adaptability to changes and traumatic events; and any indication for emotional 'cutoff.' It is important for the therapist to remind family members that the information they provide is tremendously subjective, particularly when the discussion is about the extended family. However, they need to be reminded that stories about past generations can provide useful clues for resolving emotional triangles and tensions that were not resolved in their families of origin. For example, if Hamed, an extended family member, is described as "the rebel," the therapist should search for stories being told about this label, if there were others who have been described as "the rebel," and if there were triangles being formed around family crises concerning rebellion.

In the early stages of family therapy, family members' anxiety needs to be calmed, and this may include assisting them in making an association between prevailing themes in their family's history and the development of symptoms. Further, the presenting problem may have some triangles formed around it that need to be evaluated. Clients must be informed about their interactional patterns and their functions in the family. This can be accomplished by supporting family members in understanding their problem formulation process so they can consider each family member's part with the presenting problem and family patterns.

Furthermore, therapists can ask questions to encourage differentiation, such as, "Why do you think you take your child's acting out so personally?" Family members are encourage to respond to these questions with 'I' statements to discuss their own reactions to the problem short of criticizing, or guarding against, another family member (Bowen, 1971 in Bowen, 1978). In order for clients to take responsibility for their own contributions to family relationships, clients need to learn to make personal statements about their beliefs and feelings. For example, a punitive statement like, "You are the cause of so much chaos in this family!" is shifted to, "I am worried about our relationship with each other." It is important for parents not to project their anxieties to their child using blaming tactics and to learn to 'own' their concerns and worries. Every family member needs to develop skills for focusing on 'self' to lower their anxiety so they can take responsibility for their part in problematic family interactions.

Multigenerational Lens

Bowen's multigenerational model sees families' past relational patterns continuing in the present family system (Brown, 1991). Therefore, families must be encouraged to think about how their generation is different or similar to the previous generation in dealing with their presenting problem and relational issues. For example, if the presenting problem's onset was after a death in the family, the therapist should ask the family to think about how the previous generation has dealt with grief (Brown, 1991). This is helpful because when we trace symptoms and explore interrelated issues for several generations, it becomes much harder for family members to blame each other for their inadequacies. If family members are able to understand how these patterns repeat over generations, they may be able to identify the 'automatic' responses of family members towards each other.

Detriangulation

Undoubtedly, detriangulation is a process at the heart of Bowenian family therapy. In the process of detriangulation, the first step is to help clients understand that they are 'triangled' by others and that they also attempt to triangle others. Muslim families, like many other Easterners, may not honor confidentiality, and family members may easily discuss each other's affairs with other family members. It may be also very common for individuals to try to intervene on each other's behalf in marital and parent-child relationships. This easily leads to a high level of triangulation, and family members may have a hard time identifying the triangles they participate in and how triangulation helps them bypass their anxiety.

After triangles are identified, family members need to learn about neutral communication without taking sides so the dyad can directly communicate with each other. In this way, family members can find less reactive ways to relate to each other, such as taking different positions in different emotional systems—for instance, refusing to discuss mistakes of a family member behind his/her back. Overall, the goal of any detriangling is to get family members to express neutrality about the relationship between other family members and not change other family members' relationship with each other. This neutral and calm position can potentially prevent family members from having an anxious reaction to the tension in another relationship by 'taking sides.' Detriangulation may be one of the hardest task to undertake with Muslim families, given their high level of interconnection, interdependence, and interferences in each other's lives. However, it may be one of the most important therapeutic tasks that needs to be accomplished.

Individual Family Therapy

Bowen's model can be used for working with individuals within the systemic family framework. "Coaching" is the process of giving feedback and support to adult clients who are struggling to develop differentiation skills while staying connected in their families of origin. In this process, clients use the therapist as a consultant while working on their own differentiation process. The focus is on detriangling from the family of origin patterns of relating, and it should be completely self-directed.

Bowen defined "coaching" as "family psychotherapy with one family member" (Bowen, 1971 in Bowen, 1978, p. 233). This kind of therapy teaches clients to learn about the predicable patterns of triangles. Clients are encouraged to return to their families and observe and learn about these relational patterns. Clients should also practice monitoring their own emotional reactivity with the family and should process their struggles and progress with the therapist. Throughout the family of origin coaching process, clients should use variety of ways for collecting information about their family's emotional processes and how they have inherited these patterns. Some examples are calling, writing letters, and visiting family members as well as doing research about previous generations in order to develop a systemic understanding of family patterns and triangles. The therapist helps clients with any sense of heightened anxiety and resistance that may develop in this process. A case example may help illustrate some of main concepts of this model that can be very helpful in working with Muslim families.

Case Example

The Karim family, originally from India, came to see me because of their 17-year-old daughter, Asma's, extreme anxiety symptoms and her school refusal behavior. Asma's school refusal had increased family members' reactivity towards each other, with Asma accusing her father, Ali, for his self-centered decision-making, both parents feeling angry that she had created chaos for the whole family, and her 23-year-old brother, Amin, feeling annoyed about Asma putting her family through so much worry.

My first goal with this family was to take the attention away from Asma's school refusal behavior and support the family in examining each person's roles in creating anxiety in the family system. Once I was able to broaden the family's perceptive beyond Asma's school refusal, it became apparent that the family had been dealing with some significant changes. Around the onset of Asma's school refusal and her severe anxiety symptoms, her older brother, Amin, had moved to another state to attend medical school. Amin, who was previously labeled as the defiant child, now became the golden child who would make the family proud with his academic success. Further, Mr. Karim had recently received a promotion that necessitated moving to another state. As a consequence, his wife, Mona, had to leave her extended family and was feeling very lonely. As Asma talked about her resentfulness towards her father for his decision to move to another state, and how her mother's loss of family connections made sense since she was also very connected to her cousins, a gender theme developed. All these family changes could have been related to her symptoms, but I primarily focused on the triangles in the Karim family as they were dealing with anxiety. Asma talked about her role as the triangled child in her parents' emotional interactions by discussing how her father's relocation had impacted her mother's emotional state since the move. She described both her mother's life and her life as unfulfilled and meaningless.

The level of fusion in this family was very high, with family members being highly reactive to each other. During the sessions, I noticed that their five-year-old son, Adnan, was clinging to his mother and would not explore the toys in the room. I told them that their family seemed to be closely wired to each other's feelings and that they could easily alternate between focusing on their own emotional reactions and focusing on the emotional reaction intensity of other family members. I asked some questions to understand their level of awareness about this fusion. I asked Asma if she knew that she had become her parents' emotional voice and how she should be able to talk about her own emotional needs in her family. I asked Mr. Karim to talk about the first time he had started to take Asma's symptoms personally, thinking that her complaints were only directed at him. I also asked Mrs. Karim about her son's relationship with the rest of the family before he left. Mrs. Karim reported that Amin complained of feeling smothered at home and that his relationship with his father was very conflictual. However, the relationship changed after Amin started medical school. Mr. Karim talked about how as an immigrant he struggled and worked hard so his children could accomplish their dreams and how Amin was now trying to achieve what his father dreamed of achieving for himself. From these conversations, it became apparent that all the children were somehow triangled into the emotional issues of their parents and that even though Amin and Adnan were symptom free, Asma was showing symptoms related to her parents' unresolved emotional issues.

I was able to track the Karim family members' responses to Asma's anxiety and school refusal patterns. A typical sequence was Asma refusing to go to school, Mrs. Karim getting upset about Asma's school refusal, and Asma becoming increasingly withdrawn. Mrs. Karim then would accuse Asma of being irresponsible, and Asma would accuse the family of having no understanding about her pain. After hearing about his wife's struggles, Mr. Karim would start yelling at Asma, saying how disappointed he was that she was acting so irresponsibly. Typically at this point, Mrs. Karim would intervene because she would feel bad about the situation and would make suggestions about how Asma and her father could make up. In the meantime, Asma still would not go to school but would make plans to go out shopping with her mother.

I was able to draw family members' attention to their repetitive patterns, but I also needed to find out more about multigenerational themes and connections to the present tension. Our conversation about the parents' family of origin relationship revealed powerful themes that helped me make more sense of the intense triangles between the parents and Asma. The information provided made it clear that Mr. and Mrs. Karim worrying about their daughter helped them avoid their relational issues with their own family of origins. Our main therapeutic task then was to help the parents separate their interactions with Asma from their own unresolved issues with their own families. While constructing a genogram, it became apparent that both parents were in the same middle child position as Asma, and both identified with her birth order position intensely. Mrs. Karim wanted to have a closer relationship with her daughter than she had with her own mother. However, she was able to see how the unresolved issues between her and her mother were getting in the way of setting limits with Asma. Mr. Karim was able to process, understand, and make comparison between his distanced relationship with his abusive father, who died from a heart attack, and his relationship with Asma. He just wanted a closer relationship with his daughter than he had with his own father and took Asma's disconnecting behavior personally. Therefore, the similarity between Asma's relationship with him and her symptoms and his own unresolved relational issues with his father helped him make sense of his intense reactivity to Asma's behavior. Asma was able to hear her parents' reactions and understand their own intergenerational struggles. Asma had a difficult time with the emotional shift in the family because she could no longer regulate her parents' relationship. In order to help Asma deal with this shift, I had some sessions with Asma and her brother, Amin, when he was in town so they could establish a connection as young adults dealing with the same life cycle issues. A couple of months later, Asma reported that she was in communication with Amin and that they were talking about their separate lives. After about five months of therapy, her anxiety had decreased, and she was attending school. Mr. and Mrs. Karim decided to focus on their own relationships with their own families of origin. As Asma got busier with school activities, her parents had more free time to work on their own relationships.

Summary

The essential feature of Bowen's model is that it does not concentrate on the intrapsychic experience of family members. Rather, it pays close attention to the family structure and how the family functions based on each member's systemic roles. Bowenian therapy is also more about what family members learn about the 'self in the system' and not much about how other family members are behaving and contributing to the family system dysfunction. The therapist using this model has to be careful with using a family of origin framework when working with Muslim families since they are socialized to have absolute and unquestioned loyalties to their family of origin and their relationships are extremely fused. Further, Bowen's theory does not pay attention to issues of gender, ethnicity, and class, which have a powerful effect on our contextual relationship patterns. Therefore, those who are faithful to a Bowenian framework should be very attentive to both vertical and horizontal complex family patterns especially when working with Muslim families who are from collectivistic cultural backgrounds. The role of therapists in their own families of origin and how understanding their own family patterns can connect them to their clients is the most distinctive aspect of Bowen's theory.

References

Bowen, M. (1966). The use of family theory in clinical practice. *Comprehensive Psychiatry, 7*, 345–374.

Bowen, M. (1978). *Family therapy in clinical practice.* New York: Jason Aronson.

Brown, F.H. (1991). The model. In F.H. Brown (Ed.), *Reweaving the family tapestry* (pp. 1-21). New York: Norton.

Guerin, P., Fogarty, T., Fay, L., & Kautto, J. (1996). *Working with relationship triangles.* London: Guilford.

James, K. (1989). When twos are really threes: The triangular dance in couple conflict. *Australian and New Zealand Journal of Family Therapy, 10*, 179–189.

Kerr, M., & Bowen, M. (1988). *Family evaluation: An approach based on Bowen theory.* New York: Norton.

Lerner, H. (1988). *The dance of anger.* New York: Harper & Row.

Minuchin, S. (1974). *Families & family therapy.* Cambridge: Harvard University Press.

Wylie, M.S. (1991, March-April). Family therapy's neglected Prophet. *The Family Therapy Networker*, 25–37.

CHAPTER 8

EXPERIENTIAL FAMILY THERAPY

Experiential family therapy is based on humanistic psychology and therapeutic models like Maslow, Perls, and Rogers and the communication and family systems theory of Bateson, Jackson, and Watzlavick (Becvar & Becvar, 2006). Experiential family therapy, which is based on the humanistic and experiential perspectives, developed mainly in reaction to the way behaviorism overlooked the internal and emotional experience of individuals and paid attention to only measurable and observable behaviors. Further, even though humanistic therapists liked the psychodynamic aspects of psychoanalysis, they did not like the Freudian focus on the client's past. Humanistic therapists believe that clients change when there is an authentic and truthful conversation about the experience of the client and therapist, during the session, and in the context of an empathic and honest therapeutic relationship (Nichols, 2013). This model can be very useful in working with Muslim families due to its powerful humanistic and systemic perspectives, which work well for people from collectivist cultures. In order to apply experiential family therapy in working with Muslim families, we need to have a good understanding of the main concept of family system theory along with the experiential family therapy model.

Family systems theory's main thesis is that family relationships can be improved by working with the family as a whole without pathologizing family members. In this way, family therapists do not perceive individuals as having problems or causing problems. Instead, they focus on the family system and how it needs to change in order to adapt to new rules and expectations. Experiential family therapists, like family system theorists, believe that when families get trapped in rigid and inflexible rules, the family system is the ideal level of intervention. Based on this perspective, family can either assist or prohibit the self-actualization of its members. However, experiential therapists believe that the emotional experiences of family members and the therapist have equal weight, and family therapists who have not gone through the process of self-actualization will have a difficult time helping family members with their growth process. Based on the humanistic perspective, change happens in the context of a compassionate and nonjudgmental relationship with the aid of a self-actualized therapist. Further, experiential therapists believe that families may have a hard time adjusting to change and may produce symptomatic behavior without being conscious of how they are maintaining these old self-definitions and that they need the help of a self-actualized therapist.

Traditionally, awareness of the interconnection between symptoms was an important tool for therapeutic change. However, in family systems theory, the emphasis changed from why to what, and the question became what it is about the family system that is failing to change and adapt. Experiential therapists also believe that problems are maintained by family members' behaviors within the boundaries of the family system and by the quality of experiences in the moment in the therapy room.

Systemic thinkers differ in their view of why problems are maintained in the family and unlike behavioral therapists do not see linear causality in the world. The typical example is the relationship between Naser and his wife, Sarah, in which Naser emotionally disconnects because Sarah complains. A systemic thinker does not see a causal relationship between Naser's emotional withdrawal and Sarah's complaining. Instead, a systems thinker sees Naser and Sarah participating in a collaborative pattern—Naser's emotional disconnection and Sarah's complaints—that has a reciprocal causal pattern. Experiential therapists also perceive interactions reciprocally but also believe that each person should take responsibility for his or her own emotional reactions and behaviors. The only exception is children with symptomatic behavior, which is perceived as a rather one-directional product of parental communication problems (Becvar & Becvar, 2006; Nichols, 2013). In addition, this model goes beyond other models that focus only on behavior and cognition and includes emotions as an important aspect of therapy (Nichols, 2013).

Experiential therapists and systemic therapists see the context of the whole family system creating problems and not one individual within the family system. However, experiential family therapists are more radical when it comes to who they choose to include in the session. For example, Whitaker preferred to include three generations in the session and often refused to see clients individually (Whitaker & Keith, 1982). This can be an important component for family therapy with Muslim families when multiple family members are highly involved with the problem, and being invited to the therapy session can resolve many misunderstandings among family members.

Further, just as post-modernists believe that our understanding of human behavior is restricted by many factors of which we are not conscious, experiential therapists also pay close attention to their own personal experiences and try to communicate them as authentically as possible instead of acting as objective observers.

Generally, in the mental health field, problems are seen as pathology in an individual, but to experiential therapists, problems exist because of how we communicate behaviorally, relationally, and contextually with our family members. Based on the humanistic perspective, people are inherently good and healthy. Therefore, it must be their context that creates symptomatic and problematic behavior. Experiential therapists also believe that the family members' and the therapist's experiences in the session should have equal value. Thus, even though the therapist directs family therapy, the therapist and the family can get to understand each other's experiences and values through a casual conversation. This style works well with Muslim families who are often coming from collectivistic cultures in which sharing experiences between the therapist and clients can be very helpful in changing their interactional patterns.

Compared to psychoanalysts, experiential therapists use hands-on experiences using emotionally charged interventions in the session. For instance, Satir uses family sculpting (Satir & Baldwin, 1983), and Whitaker uses emotional confrontation (Neil & Kniskern, 1982). They use candid, honest reframing to create emotional and communication shifts in families. However, they are less directive in changing a particular problematic behavior (Nichols, 2013).

EXPERIENTIAL FAMILY THERAPY CORE ASSUMPTIONS

The central framework of experiential family therapists and humanistic psychology is basically the same. However, experiential family therapy uses the family systems framework and states that individuals move towards self-actualization in a relationally healthy environment. On the other hand, an individual's growth can be restricted in an unsafe and non-expressive environment. If individuals are in a safe and expressive environment, they can experience real intimacy and true individuality with others and communicate accurately and authentically in intimate relationships. Thus, the role the experiential therapist plays is crucial because psychological congruency and affection can be modeled by the therapist to help individuals in families act authentically in relations with others and mutually support each other's growth (Becvar & Becvar, 2006; Nichols, 2013; Satir, 1972).

Experiential family therapists believe that it is the client's unique expression of strengths that enhances his or her personal growth. They emphasize that the catalyst for family relational change is the therapist's sincere and authentic expression of his or her own unique strengths and forming a warm connection with the client (Baldwin & Satir, 1987). It seems like the trust and sincere regard for individuals is a good instrument of change for clients. Experiential therapists use behavioral, affective, and cognitive training to enhance relational intimacy and clients' precision of perception and expression. The intervention is often at the relational and system's level to help family members form intimate relationships with each other in the family system.

HEALTHY AND PROBLEMATIC FAMILY DEVELOPMENT

As mentioned before, the humanistic tradition is the base for experiential family therapists' therapeutic work. They assume that children have an inner drive to self-actualize with a sufficient amount of encouragement and support and the slightest level of authoritarian social and relational controls. They believe that emotionally healthy families find appropriate ways to cope with stress and understand each family member's emotional needs. Healthy families are also able to recognize each other's personal styles and communicate about them effectively. These families are good at combining their resources in order to solve problems and meet everyone's needs.

Experiential therapists assume that relational problems in families are often related to inflexible, endless corrective rules, roles, and unreasonable schedules pressuring them to negate and alter their ordinary experiences. Family members try to behave according to these rigid family rules in order to avoid rejection. When family members behave in certain ways that are contradictory to the family's expectations, and their own subjective experiences are denied, an inconsistency develops between self and life experiences.

For individuals who experience these major inconsistencies when they form their own families and have their own children, the restrictions they have internalized and adapted from their own family of origin parents, such as 'Don't be mad,' 'Don't be afraid,' 'Don't be unhappy,' 'Be good,' 'Be cheerful,' 'Don't protest,' and 'Don't argue,' may influence them to deny their family members' strong emotions the same way their own feelings were denied. These authentic but rejected strong emotions like fear, anger, or sadness become projected to a child through the scapegoating process. Thus, a child may be singled out, labeled as 'mad,' 'sad,' 'sick,' or 'bad,' and his anger, fear, or sadness will be denied. In adulthood, then, these unprocessed emotions and unresolved feelings from childhood need to be resolved if emotional growth is to occur.

Treatment

Experiential family therapists are not interested in resolving specific problems and mostly focus on the emotional growth of each family member. Personal development necessitates growing self-esteem, self-awareness, self-responsibility, and self-actualization. When an individual becomes more self-aware, a genuine and accurate appreciation of strengths as well as weaknesses, abilities, and potentials, along with vulnerabilities and needs, becomes possible. With a higher level of self-esteem, individuals can better evaluate their sense of self in meaningful relationships and other personal and spiritual contexts. Increased self-responsibility helps individuals not deny others' personal experiences or characteristics and become accepting and accountable for their own personal experiences. Self-actualization is exploring one's true potentials; owning all aspects of human self; processing unresolved emotions; trying to be accountable for all actions; honoring other's experiences; and communicating needs and desires in a consistent and authentic way. Experiential therapy helps clients change the influence of larger contextual and developmental issues, which maintain the interactional problems in the family system.

The methods experiential family therapists use to change families' interactional patterns are innovative and emotionally intense. They use creativity and non-rational methods to help families deal with developmental barriers for personal growth. According to this model, therapeutic change happens when the therapeutic relationship is authentic and the therapist pays close attention to the depth of clients' emotional experiences during the session. Therefore, emotional congruency, warmth, and a nonjudgmental way of relating to the client are important source of healing.

Personal disclosure is important in order to deepen the therapeutic coalition and assist with clients' personal growth. Clients are encouraged to experience a wide range of emotions in the session to connect them to their past and present life. These new emotional experiences can be used to assess the maintenance of problem-saturated belief systems in order to change their behavioral patterns and attain a higher level of personal growth.

It is important to conceptualize the specific work of Carl Whitaker and Virginia Satir, the founders of their experiential approaches to family therapy, so their family therapy style can be used in working with Muslim families. They developed their separate approaches to working with families in the late 1950s, but they both showed great passion for utilizing family therapy and emphasized the uselessness of individual therapy.

Carl Whitaker

Carl Whitaker had the most fascinating, explicit theory about the central role of the scapegoating process in problem development, even though he was critical of the inflexible theoretical frameworks in what they called effective therapy (Mitten & Cinnell, 2004). He believed that a scapegoat was the person with mental health symptoms who became the target of all the anger, criticism, and negative feelings within the family so the family did not have to deal with their real relational problems. For example, parents deny their conflict because if they acknowledge it, it may lead to violence, separation, or divorce, so all the negative emotions related to the conflict get transferred to a child, and the child shows psychological symptoms. One of Whitaker's major assumptions was that families resist engaging in family therapy because their participation means they are accepting the identified patient only as a person revealing broader relational difficulties in the family. Family resistance also occurs because they are afraid of being forced to deal with wider family issues. Whitaker also believed that families may want therapists to solve their issues and may have a hard time accepting responsibilities for change.

Whitaker believed the effectiveness of family therapy depends on two confrontational interventions: the battle for structure and the battle for initiative. With the battle for structure, the therapist is in charge of structuring the sessions and asking all family members to attend all therapy sessions. With the battle for initiative, the major obligation is on the family for what gets discussed and processed. The two interventions help the family resolve their denied difficulties and increase the chances for challenging and changing the role of the scapegoating process. Further, Whitaker was more interested in 'being with' families and had no interest in using techniques in resolving ongoing conflicts. Whitaker intuitively used self-disclosure and what he termed "craziness" (Whitaker & Malone, 1953; Whitaker & Ryan, 1989). Whittaker's understanding and insight about family functioning had a significant influence on the development of family therapy. His style is useful in working with Muslim families because of the emphasis on whole family functioning and relational strengths.

VIRGINIA SATIR

Virginia Satir believed that personal growth should be the main goal of family therapy (Satir, 1988; Baldwin & Satir, 1987). This often meant helping clients increase their self-esteem and make their own choices, as well as become more responsible and congruent, in order to experience harmony between feelings, thought, and behavior. She was also an advocate for helping clients attain self-determination, deal with their unfinished business, and get away from the impact of past negative events.

Satir's approach focused on interaction with the current family system, as well as their relationships with members of their families of origin. Satir used an iceberg metaphor for conceptualizing the intrapsychic system and assumed that the current interactional patterns in families were the observable part of a symbolic iceberg. She discussed six hierarchical layers: having primary feelings (happiness or sadness); having feelings about other's feelings (worrying about being mad); having opinions (belief systems and values); having expectations of self and others; having the desire to belong; and having a sense of self (Satir, 1988). Satir asked explicit questions about these hierarchical layers because she believed these self-contained feelings, attitudes, desires, and hopes triggered all visible problematic behavior patterns.

Virginia Satir discussed the impact of evolving problematic communication styles of blaming, placating, distracting, and computing where family members deny strong emotions and cannot clearly communicate their needs with each other. Blaming is used when family members do not take responsibility to resolve their conflict. They use judging, comparing, complaining, and bullying others without taking responsibility for their own role in the problem. Placating is using constant diffusion without resolving any conflicts and is characterized by peacemaking, not discussing differences, blocking conflict, and being excessively 'nice.' Distracting is avoiding to resolve conflicts and is characterized by trying to change the subject, remaining quiet, acting helpless, or pretending to misunderstand. Computing is avoiding emotional engagement with others and may involve using rational and analytical approaches, preaching, using moral judgments, expecting to win intellectual arguments, and not acknowledging all the emotions involved with these arguments.

"Leveling" is a communicational style used by Satir as an adaptive style for promoting resolution of conflicts. It promotes congruency of verbal and non-verbal communications, transparency, sincerity, and truthfulness. According to Satir, if family members would use leveling as the main form of communication, then family members' personal growth would be cultivated. Satir's therapy involves delicately modeling and teaching family members to level with each other. She often encouraged families to use what she called "temperature reading" and put time aside to relate to each other by showing appreciation, soliciting information, resolving relational problems, and discussing dreams and hope for the future.

Furthermore, in order to increase verbal communication, Satir also believed in the use of touch to facilitate personal growth within family therapy and asked family members to sit closer, hold hands, and touch each other in the session and encouraged family members to do the same at home. While Satir also used other techniques like family sculpting, using metaphors, storytelling, and externalizing internal process as therapeutic techniques, using metaphors and storytelling may be more useful techniques for Muslim families than sculpturing and externalizing internal process, which may not make sense to Eastern families that view therapy as a highly structured process of learning from the therapist's expertise.

One of Satir's important techniques was a process to help clients change their maladaptive relational rules into adaptive ones and involved changing 'should' to 'can'; changing 'never' or 'always' to 'sometimes'; and helping clients with identifying possibilities. For instance, "I should never talk about my feelings" becomes "I can sometimes talk about my feelings when I want others to know how I want to be treated."

The therapist's use of 'self' is an important component of change in Satir's model. She examined different aspects of the self she called "self-mandala," viewing them as a connected circles that contain the physical parts of self at the center and then the sensual, nutritional, intellectual, emotional, interactional, contextual, and spiritual around the center (Carr, 2006). Satir's concept of self-mandala is useful in identifying clients' personal powers, which can reveal the interdependence and connections between different parts of the self. According to Satir, self-actualized therapists and clients practice self-care and try to attain higher self-esteem, have a sense of independence and self-sufficiency, act responsibly, and are congruent in their relationships with others. Therapists and clients can accomplish all of these by maintaining harmony between the eight aspects of self. A clinical example reveals the usefulness of this model in working with Muslim families.

Case Example

Afra, age 16, had been sexually abused by her mother's brother, Ahmed, for five years between the ages of 10 and 15. She told her mother, Aminah, a year earlier, but her mother did not believe her because Afra had a habit of lying even about important things, and her mother believed that Ahmed was a "religious man" who would not simply do what Afra accused him of doing. He had provided financial and emotional support for Aminah when she was leaving her abusive husband. A few weeks before our first therapy session, Afra told a teacher at school, and the teacher discussed this with Aminah. She later confronted Afra again, and the younger sister, Amal, confessed that Ahmed had touched her as well. Aminah confronted Ahmed, but he denied the allegations. Social services intervened and pressed charges against Ahmed, and Aminah was asked to seek family therapy. During the first phase of therapy, I noticed that Afra was very sad that she did not have a close relationship with her mother and about the fact that her mother didn't believe her when she told her about her uncle. Aminah was very distanced and defensive, and when we discussed this issue she used many examples of her daughter's lying behavior and accused Afra of reading too much into the situation. Afra felt that her mother was not validating her feelings. This is a clear example of the cyclical process that Satir identified as the basis of problem formation in families. Afra seemed to have low self-esteem, so she did not communicate congruently how she was feeling, which enhanced her low self-esteem even more. On the other hand, Aminah felt ashamed of what had happened but was unable to hear criticism, so she assumed a blaming position as well.

This perception of mother-as-villain in interfamilial abuse cases is not unusual. Mothers have been viewed as 'responsible' in a number of ways. Research has shown that one of the most important components of recovery for incest abuse victims is whether they are heard and believed by their mother upon disclosure (Kim, Talbot, & Cicchetti, 2009). Most significantly, that the abuse has occurred at all has been conceptualized as a result of the mother's collusion with the offender, her possible passive-dependent personality, and/or her "psychological absence" as both a mother and a wife (Kim, Talbot, & Cicchetti, 2009). Satir, on the other hand, outlines a better way of looking at the healthy potential for Aminah's relationship with Afra. Based on Satir's perspective, it is possible that Aminah's resistance to connect with Afra's pain is because of her fear of entering a scary place. There may exist lots of unacceptable feelings that block Aminah's growth and potentials as Afra's mother. Having been exposed as a mother, and lacking in good judgment since she trusted the abuser with her children, made her feel that her role as nurturer and protector had been relinquished. Perhaps her blaming pose with Afra around issues of trust and responsibility was an attempt to hide from herself and the depth and painfulness of her own guilt and shame for feeling untrustworthy and irresponsible with Afra. Based on this framework I tried to make it safe for Aminah to express her full range of feelings about what happened to Afra—her sadness, guilt, and anger; her fears of having failed as a mother. According to Satir, by helping Aminah tolerate these unacceptable feelings, perhaps Aminah could begin to connect more genuinely with her daughter.

One of the clues Satir advocates using to assess how authentically and fully people are communicating their feelings with one another is their tone of voice and body language (Satir & Baldwin, 1983). Aminah's tone of voice was cold and defensive, and her posture was blaming and distant. I tried to make her feel safe so she could share these unacceptable feelings that were adding to her low self-esteem. This involved blocking the repetitive incongruent sequence and supporting Aminah to get closer to her unacceptable feelings. I stated that she could empathize with her daughter's pain as a mother because she also wanted to protect her children and saw that as the number one priority. Satir believed that self-disclosure is appropriate if used as a way to facilitate a genuine connection with people. So I helped Aminah share how she felt when she allowed herself to believe Afra was abused and validated her pain as evidenced by her tears.

I also invited Aminah to feel more fully her pain about Afra being sexually abused by someone Aminah trusted. Aminah's close relationship with her brother and how he helped her get a divorce from her abusive husband, as well as family loyalties, were all discussed. At several points, Aminah tried to defend her brother, saying that "he is a very good-hearted person, and he is not an all-bad person." I was able to challenge Aminah and separate these issues, stating that he could be a good person but that he did something bad to Afra and that she deserved the acknowledgment from her mother. Aminah was encouraged to allow herself to feel the pain in Afra's presence so both Aminah and Afra could start the healing process.

In the last part of therapy, Aminah and Afra were both experiencing more self-congruent communication with each other. They were more willing to tolerate their own and each other's tears and pain. In addition to supporting and encouraging the expression of the pain nonanxiously, I discussed the possible healthy intention of Afra's misbehaviors. It was explained to them that this might be her way of protesting the disconnection from her mother. She may have been attempting to be noticed and attended to by Aminah but in a way that generated negative, not positive, attention. Both Aminah and Afra were encouraged to give each other hugs and spend time alone together. Over the next few weeks, they both spent time with each other, and Afra got a chance to talk about the abuse in detail, and Aminah listened to her story without doubting Afra was telling the truth. They continued to receive therapy in different configurations (individual, dyadic, and family including Amal in sessions).

The sexual victimization of children can create a significant amount of emotionality and reactivity within and between the offended, the non-offending family members, and even the mental health professionals who are trying to help the family. All those involved experience, to some degree, a sense of violation and powerlessness. All are faced with multiple decisions, and all these decisions can be equally hard. The discussion of sexual abuse is especially hard if the perpetrator is a family member in collectivistic cultures when family members rely on each other for support and family loyalties are supposed to be very strong. This topic is even harder to discuss for Muslim families given the fact that a girl who has been raped may have a hard time being married as an adult because virginity is still very much valued in Muslim societies. Therefore, it is more important to discuss these issues and separate them out so families don't get stuck in a vicious cycle of shame and blame and are able to concentrate on holding the perpetrator and not the victim responsible for this act of disgrace and degradation.

Virginia Satir was interested in helping family members arrive at a new meaning of themselves and each other that offered more possibility for growth and connections. Her compassion and nonblaming attitude towards people's unhealthy patterns enabled her to invite people to see that they have many more choices about how to connect with themselves and with one another than they were aware. She noted that "it is in honoring all parts of ourselves and being free to accept those parts that we lay the groundwork for high self-esteem" (Satir, 1988, p. 34).

Summary

The experiential family therapy perspective is based on viewing people as inherently healthy and growth oriented, which has two obvious clinical advantages. First, the assumption of a healthy core invites the therapist to move closer to people, even when they show many signs of dysfunction. The therapeutic context becomes a process of uncovering the underlying health rather than cautiously waiting for the 'real' pathology to emerge.

The closer the therapist gets, the clearer the client's health and growth potential become. Second, the assumption of and focus in therapy on positive intentions, in and of itself, creates space for people to begin to see for themselves the possibility of healthier alternative outcomes (Satir, 1988). Experiential therapy advocates for approaches in therapy that transform impasses by lending people acceptance for what has been, vision for something different, and courage to make that change. The concepts of this theory are refreshing and very useful for Muslim families and will be very much appreciated because of their humanistic and transforming nature.

REFERENCES

Baldwin, M., & Satir, V. (1987). *The use of self in therapy.* New York: Hawthorn.

Becvar, D.S., & Becvar, R.J. (2006). *Family therapy: A systemic integration.* Boston, MA: Pearson.

Carr, A. (2006). *Family therapy: Concepts, process and practice* (2nd ed.). New York: John Wiley & Sons Ltd.

Kim, J., Talbot, N., & Cicchetti, D. (2009). Child abuse. *Neglect, 33*, 362–371.

Mitten, T., & Cinnell, G. (2004). The core variables of symbolic-experiential family therapy. *Journal of Marital and Family Therapy, 30*, 467–478. doi:http://dx.doi.org/10.1111/j.1752-0606.2004.tb01256.x

Neill, J.R., & Kniskern, D.P. (1982). *From psyche to system: The evolving therapy of Carl Whitaker.* New York: Guilford.

Nichols, M. (2013). *Family therapy: Concepts and methods* (10th ed.). Boston: Pearson.

Satir, V. (1972). *Peoplemaking.* Palo Alto: Science and Behavior.

Satir, V. (1988). *The new peoplemaking.* Palo Alto: Science and Behaviour.

Satir, V., & Baldwin, M. (1983). *Satir step by step: A guide to creating change in families.* Palo Alto: Science and Behavior.

Whitaker, C., & Keith, D.V. (1982). Symbolic-experiential family therapy. In D.P. Kniskern & J.R. Neill (Eds.), *From psyche to system: The evolving therapy of Carl Whitaker* (pp. 330–378). New York: Guilford.

Whitaker, C., & Malone, T. (1953). *The roots of psychotherapy.* New York: Blakinson.

Whitaker, C., & Ryan, M. (1989). *Midnight musings of a family therapist.* New York: Norton.

Chapter 9

NARRATIVE FAMILY THERAPY

People's problems, and examining family members' identities and roles as constructed through family relations, culture, and history, have always been part of the common themes for family therapy even though family therapy theories are very diverse. Family members' narratives, centering on their life stories, and based on post-modern viewpoints, have become an influential family therapy framework over the past several decades (Freeman & Couchonnal, 2006; Nichols, 2013). In this approach, the therapist's role in the process of therapy is based on social constructionist ideas, which is a major paradigm shift in the family therapy field (Legg & Stagaki, 2002; Nichols, 2013). Social constructionism's main ideas center around understanding the processes people use to explain, describe, rationalize, and eventually view themselves and the world around them (Legg and Stagaki, 2002). Based on this post-modern perspective, narrative theory values multiple realities and experiences and rejects the idea of a universal truth. Furthermore, clients are experts about their own life stories, and their perspectives are valued and honored. In this approach, the therapist's view of the problem is perceived as simply one perspective and not necessarily the main or the privileged one (Legg and Stagaki, 2002; Nichols, 2013).

Further, the therapist asks for a family's narrative based on their contextual framework and connection to the past, which can provide meaningful information for family members to identify and understand their problems and challenges. However, the meanings people assign to their own stories and their family's narratives are always created and constructed based on the society they live in. Societies almost always value particular ways of being and relating and give those more status and devalue many others. Societies do not validate the life experiences of those who do not conform to the dominant cultural stories, even though these culturally sanctioned lifestyles and values have often changed throughout history. Minority groups, people with disabilities either physically or mentally, or people with different gender role configurations may have their stories less validated by the society they live in (Freeman & Couchonnal, 2006). When people realize that their life stories don't fit the societal norms and expectations, they may hide many important aspects of their personal histories and stories.

The role that society and culture have in creating personal struggles is one of the most important emphases of narrative therapy, which makes this model applicable to work with ethnically and culturally diverse families (Freeman & Couchonnal, 2006). This model can be very effective in working with Muslim families when cultural metaphors can exert a great deal of influence on family dynamics. Any destructive or marginalizing cultural narratives can be identified and deconstructed by narrative therapists in order to build more empowering and inspiring cultural stories. When people feel that they are stuck in meaningless and incongruent stories, they often try to get professional help. Narrative therapists, then, can assist individuals and families with creating more rewarding and genuine personal stories that are less influenced by main societal narratives (Nichols, 2013). A collaborative method of identifying and externalizing challenges through a meaningful therapeutic conversation can change family members' experience of themselves and alter the impact of social influences. It also deconstructs the story's implication or importance; accentuates the way personal and family strengths can be highlighted; and eventually creates the formation of other stories. Narrative therapy can be one of the most clinically useful models in working with Muslim families living in Western countries because of the powerful societal narratives defining Muslims and their family interactions in a negative light. This is also a very useful model in working with families living in Muslim-dominated countries because of the way family interactions are also judged and perceived by their societies.

Narrative Therapy Techniques

Creating trust and establishing a healthy connection with the client or the family are the basis for any therapeutic approach. Listening and validating clients' stories are the hallmark of narrative therapy. Active and attentive listening to clients' prevailing family or cultural narratives tells us a lot about how families describe their issues, how they try to resolve them, how they view themselves, and their perception of the process of change (Freeman & Couchonnal, 2006). It may be simple to listen to families tell their stories, but therapists are responsible for their own level of consciousness about their own biases as they listen and try to understand the sources of the problems in the family story. Therefore, narrative therapists' own personal and cultural narratives and their previous life experiences need to be explored first in order to prevent the influence of their own life stories on the significant aspects of clients' stories (Nichols, 2013). Another important aspect of the narrative model is recognizing that clients have the right to understand their own issues and define their own reality the way it makes sense to them. Therefore, the therapist must embrace a naïve approach and let the clients be the experts in understanding their own life stories. In this way, the client and therapist can fully collaborate and work together, coauthoring a new narrative based on the reciprocated consideration of the client's issues and challenges (Nichols, 2013). Further, even though the therapist and client are collaborating, the therapist must be the one who organizes the discussion and creates room for novel stories and meanings. Narrative therapists use externalizing techniques by asking clients to give their struggle a name or title to help them separate their dominant stories from themselves (Freeman & Couchonnal, 2006) because they believe that people are not their problems and should not be defined by their problems. This externalization process aids clients in viewing themselves as separate from these dominant stories and helps them concentrate on those exceptional experiences that allow them to separate themselves from problems in their relationships. Therapists who use externalization try to unconditionally support clients to name, symbolize, or even humanize their problems so they can see them as separate entities (Nichols, 2013). For example, Ammar is not angry, but influenced by anger. This technique decreases Ammar's powerlessness and offers him ways that he can change his behavior. Another technique called "mapping" encourages the therapist to ask questions to find out about how the problem is influencing the client's life (Nichols, 2013). Asking Ammar a question like, "How does anger get you in trouble?" can help Ammar utilize his own resources and influence his own problem at hand. Further, narrative therapists have adopted the deconstructive technique to undermine cultural hierarchies and the dominant societal norms and to help clients find an alternative way to examine their problem-saturated stories and change their perspectives (Boston, 2005). The ultimate goal of narrative therapy, then, is the deconstruction of clients' dominant stories, which is also an essential prelude to the reconstruction of new stories. Narrative therapists listen to clients' stories, searching for contradictions, omissions, exceptions, or any possible hidden meanings within the story that can be used to help clients overcome obstacles in their lives and change their behaviors (Nichols, 2013).

Therapists may use their observations to formulate rhetorical or circular questions such as, "What would have to happen to change this story's ending?" In fact, deconstruction helps therapists "read between the lines" when listening to a specific story and create a new perspective in order to begin the authoring of a new story (Nichols, 2013). The core of narrative technique is seeking out and utilizing individual strengths (Freeman & Couchonnal, 2006). It is critical for the client and therapist to collaborate and redefine challenges and deconstruct the story because together they can discover unrecognized capabilities and strengths. The therapist, then, discusses these 'unique outcomes' and asks clients questions related to overcoming a specific problem by themselves or when the problem was not as evident or demanding.

It is challenging to find exceptions to the dominant story because clients often have an easier time focusing on all the negatives and have a hard time finding strengths or perceiving of themselves as competent. In some situations, the therapist may share a story about a public figure who has overcome similar problems and then speculate about the client's own exception stories (Freeman & Couchonnal, 2006). A new story will be created if the therapist can identify exceptions and strengths. Our life stories are impacted by our culture, history, and context, but we can also change that narrative and rewrite a new story. Further, narrative therapists can assist clients in developing new meanings and clarifying prevailing stories.

Narrative therapy helps families work together to build a new story that focuses on strengths and meaning. The new story, then, reflects on how the family is and how it wants to be. This is usually done by using reframing and offering families different ways to think about the problem to provide them with new possibilities for resolving problems and recovery (Freeman & Couchonnal, 2006; Nichols, 2013). These new behaviors can be supported in therapy sessions; by journaling and developing rituals on their own time; or by associating with supportive people who can endorse their new story (Freeman & Couchonnal, 2006; Nichols, 2013). The therapist can highlight the development of new stories, either by discussing it in the session or by sending clients a letter (Nicholas, 2013).

One of the greatest strengths of narrative therapy is its flexibility, because it can be easily used in conjunction with other family therapy models and with culturally diverse families. For example, family systems models (Dallos, 2004; Woodcock, 2001), attachment theory (Dallos, 2004), strategic therapy, and even solution-focused modalities (Freeman & Couchonnal, 2006) are models that have been successfully combined with narrative therapy. This model has shown effectiveness when used with individuals, couples, and families, and even groups (Jones, 2004). Further, narrative approaches can be used in conjunction with art and play therapies treating low self-esteem and helping children and adolescents learn coping skills (Wood & Frey, 2003). This approach may not be effective in working with individuals suffering from some sorts of brain damage, periodic psychosis, or mental retardation (Freeman & Couchonnal, 2006).

Conceivably, assessing narrative therapy's effectiveness can be a great limitation of this model because the transformation of a personal story cannot be operationalized and measured. The usefulness of narrative therapy with individuals, couples, and families has not been fully supported by research. Nevertheless, researchers and clinicians have explored the concept of coherence to measure and evaluate client progress (Dallos, 2004). Coherence of a new narrative can be measured by linearity, stability, and relevance, as well as lack of self-contradictory statements. Much of the research about coherence has used attachment theory to show that adults can raise secure, attached children if they are able to tell coherent stories about their own childhood experiences with their parents (Dallos, 2004). In addition, even helping family members to learn to tell more coherent stories in a clinical setting can be very beneficial (Byng-Hall, 1998). Therefore, assessing clients' stories by using the coherence criteria can be helpful in identifying areas of narrative incoherence. It also allows therapists and clients to observe and examine the impact of these narratives in altering and changing clients' thought process. A case example can reveal the usefulness of this model with Muslim families.

Case Example

Sarah was a 45-year-old woman with anxiety and depression symptoms. She was experiencing insomnia, which caused her to get tired easily and very often sleep during the day. Sarah's symptoms had been present for four years, but prior to seeking help, her symptoms became unbearable. Sarah is from Palestine and lost her husband, Amin, when he was crossing the border to Israel to buy milk for their youngest child, Yaser. The body of her husband, the father of her three children, was never recovered. After this incident, Sarah quit her job as a nurse to concentrate on raising her children. The family lived in the refugee camp in the Gaza Strip before they moved to the US. The oldest child, Hashim (17), was a kind and responsible boy with a good relationship with his mother; even though he would often fight with his sister, Samia (15), and get in trouble for fights at school. Samia did not have many friends, was spending most of her time outside school at home, and was the main caretaker for her younger brother, Yaser (6), after school and on weekends, when her mother was very often sleeping. Sarah had been on prescription medication for anxiety and depression for the past two years. Listening to the family's stories revealed that unresolved grief around Sarah's husband's death was their main struggle. They did not have many social interactions with the Muslim community, and Sarah claimed that she had tried to socialize with people but felt that she "didn't belong."

Sarah tried really hard to concentrate on her children's welfare and making sure they didn't see any sign of grieving or sadness. She called Hashim and Samia the "rocks I hold on to" and was very appreciative of their compassion and commitment to the family after their father died. On the other hand, it was becoming more difficult for Sarah to "keep it together." Sarah felt that her depressive symptoms were impacting her ability to be emotionally present and care for her children.

Hashim seemed preoccupied with news about Palestinians' struggles. He would constantly listen to the news and become frustrated about the situation in Palestine. He would get very agitated and opinionated whenever the topic of conflict between Israel and Palestinian was raised. When anyone would challenge him about his views, Hashim would claim that "I owe it to my father" to "spread the truth about the situation at home." He idolized his father and often spoke of him as his hero and as a man who trained him to "be strong" and "to be a real man." Even though Samia was eight years old when her father was martyred, she often talked about their time together before he died. She stated frequently that "I talk to my dad" but wouldn't share the conversations with her brother or mother. Samia was upset about the way her brother and mother were dealing with her father's death. She felt that they had "forgotten him" and that she was the "only one who still cared." She would get upset with people calling her father a hero because Samia believed her father's death was "a waste." This was a constant source of conflict between Samia and Hashim.

In working with them, it became apparent Sarah, Samia, and Hashim had processed the events of the prior five years very differently. They were all dealing with the impact of a great personal loss, which was somehow buried under people's lack of understanding of the daily struggles of Palestinians. The fact that Amin went to buy milk for Yaser and got killed added layers of guilt, and then not being able to bury the body added ambiguity to their unfinished story, and they never had any sense of closure. Helping the family uncover their personal stories of loss and helping them deal with their buried grief were some of the main goals of family therapy.

One of my main challenges was for Sarah to come up with her own narrative about someone who was heartbroken about the loss of her husband, instead of viewing herself as a victim of a meaningless and never-ending war. Hashim felt that being loyal to his father meant not voicing his frustration or expressing his grief and instead directing his energy into being angry, frustrated, and distanced. Therefore, for Hashim it was necessary to create a new story where he was not a replacement for his father as a strong man, but as a son and a brother who was deeply hurt by his father's tragic death. Samia was convinced that she was the only one in the family who had addressed her loss, but I needed to help her recognize that her brother and mother also missed her father and that there was no need for her to continue carrying her family's grief. Finally, all family members needed to acknowledge Amin's death and recognize the fact that they all shared a sense of loss and need to help each other grieve.

The US public debate and people's lack of understanding about the unfair and unbalanced conflict between Israel and Palestine seemed to create a great deal of pain and powerlessness for a family who wanted to commemorate a personal loss. In helping this family heal, it was important to use deconstruction techniques to help them separate the Palestinian struggle for continuing to fight for a just cause from their personal grief. I helped the family write a story about their father and husband and tried to separate their loss from how other Palestinian families have also been influenced by these continuous struggles.

I particularly helped Samia and Hashim recognize and deal with their personal losses. This was very helpful for Samia because she was no longer feeling alone in dealing with her grief. It was very helpful to all of them to tell stories about Amin as a father and husband, and not as a war causality. It was also important to process their grief before Yaser become older and realized his father had been killed trying to buy milk for him and ultimately might blame himself for something that was not his fault. My ultimate goal was to help each one of them re-author a new family story that included all of their personal losses so they could give themselves permission to grieve and begin the healing process. This family's grieving process was complicated because they did not have a body to bury and did not have a designated grave or memorial. Thus, they needed to find a way to honor their painful story. So I encouraged them to cooperatively create a ritual to honor Amin's death. They talked about planting a tree in the mosque's backyard, and all agreed that this would be a good idea. The main point was for them to collaborate and create a personal memorial that could help them grieve and contemplate, and the mosque seemed to be the best place for them. Hashim was going to lead the memorial ceremony, and his mother and sister would read poems in Arabic. In this way, they all collaborated to build a story that honored their husband and father. I met with the family after the tree-planting ceremony at the mosque. They all talked about this shared experience that hopefully served to support their new evolving family narrative.

Summary

In the epistemology of post-modernism that narrative therapy embraces, the concept of 'relative truth' is central. It uses the same scientific approaches for exploring, observing, and gathering evidence to either upkeep or refute the dominant narrative. Narrative therapy treats clients as experts in their own stories. The therapist, however, can still offer clients expertise, trying to help them explore the impact of their story on their behavior and relationships. Further, since being neutral and objective is not possible within the social constructionism paradigm, narrative therapists discuss their own opinions about stories they may favor and give credibility to one version of a client's story and not the other ones. It may even be appropriate for narrative therapists to disclose their own stories. Further, narrative therapists try to help clients recognize their own strengths and externalize their problems, but they also hold each person responsible for authoring their own stories and assigning meaning to them. Finally, narrative therapy deliberately considers how society and the dominant culture play a significant role in how people understand their own struggles, which makes this model a powerful perspective in working with Muslim families.

References

Boston, P. (2005). Doing deconstruction. *Journal of Family Therapy, 27*, 272–275. doi:http://dx.doi.org/10.1111/j.1467-6427.2005.00316.x

Byng-Hall, J. (1998). Evolving ideas about narrative: Re-editing the re-editing of family mythology. *Journal of Family Therapy, 20*, 133–141.

Dallos, R. (2004). Attachment narrative therapy: Integrating ideas from narrative and attachment theory in systemic family therapy with eating disorders. *Journal of Family Therapy, 26*, 40–65. doi:http://dx.doi.org/10.1111/j.1467-6427.2004.00266.x

Freeman, E.M., & Couchonnal, G. (2006). Narrative and culturally based approaches in practice with families. *Families in Society: The Journal of Contemporary Social Services, 87*, 198–208.

Jones, A.C. (2004). Transforming the story: Narrative applications to a stepmother support group. *Families in Society: The Journal of Contemporary Social Services, 85*, 129–138.

Legg, C., & Stagaki, P. (2002). How to be a postmodernist: A user's guide to postmodern rhetorical practices. *Journal of Family Therapy, 24*, 385–401. doi:http://dx.doi.org/10.1111/1467-6427.00226

Nichols, M.P. (2013). *Family therapy: Concepts and methods* (10th ed.). Boston: Pearson Education.

Wood, G.G., & Frey, A. (2003). Helping children cope: A narrative approach to the life space interview. *School Social Work Journal, 27*, 57–78.

Woodcock, J. (2001). Threads from the labyrinth: Therapy with survivors of war and political oppression. *Journal of Family Therapy, 23*, 136–154. doi:http://dx.doi.org/10.1111/1467-6427.00174

Chapter 10

CONTEXTUAL FAMILY THERAPY

Contextual family therapy developed in the mid-twentieth century. The interests of its founder, Iván Böszörményi-Nagy, focused on treating severe mental disorders by going beyond individual psychopathology and looking into family interactions (Carey, 2007). Böszörményi-Nagy noticed destructive patterns of family interactions are often passed on through generations. This perspective helped him formulate the contextual model, which equipped family therapy with new theoretical principles and practical applications.

The core of contextual theory rests on two principles. First, all family members are affected by each other's actions or inactions. Second, the quality of family members' relationships is inseparable from the responsible consideration of the relationships' impact on others (Fowers & Wagner, 1997). This approach can be used in working with Muslim families given its comprehensive approach to family pathology and the solutions proposed by this model as well as its relational emphasis, which works well with collectivistic family dynamics. Contextual theory proposed four interconnected but not equitable or reducible to each other dimensions of relational reality: facts, individual psychology, transactions, and relational ethics. These are both a guide for therapeutic interventions and a theoretical concept.

Facts

The first dimension, facts, consists of factual reality and biological determinates that we have limited or no control over. Many events and incidents occur in families or societies, such as immigrating to another country, becoming unemployed, multicultural adoptions, births, deaths, and ethnic and religious conflicts, that impact the family's relationships, change interaction patterns, and deeply affect both individual and family goals. Along with biological and historical destinies this can create conflicts within the family that, if unresolved, can become factual realities, creating grounds for "split-loyalty" (Krasner, Joyce, 1995, p. 19). When more than one generation of the family become involved in such unresolved conflict, the impact of the behavior of that one generation becomes a legacy, passed down to the next generation. These events are termed "created realities" (Fowers & Wagner, 1997).

This multigenerational perspective is a significant aspect of contextual theory and has become probably one of the most important contributions of Böszörményi-Nagy to this model. It creates new interpretations for understanding family development and interactions. Shpungina (2009) explains how limitations of civil rights of Jews in the Russian Empire in the eighteenth and nineteenth centuries, for example, resulted in the formation of closer bonds within families, which have been passed down through generations. These traits are present in many families of their offspring until now. Another example is the importance of family loyalties to tribal culture in previous centuries, which still defines relationships for many Muslim families in the Middle East.

INDIVIDUAL PSYCHOLOGY

The second dimension of contextual theory refers to the inner world of each family member and "includes cognitions, emotions, fantasies and other symbolic processes" (Piercy, Sprenkle, & Wetchler, 1996, p. 28). Opposite "to the systemic approach, where the individual was often lost" (Gangamma, 2008, p. 11), contextual theory states that the same processes affect the development of families and individual family members. People have different strengths and limitations and are different in their cognitive and coping abilities and techniques. In the therapeutic setting, "failing to see individual's personal concerns, thoughts, wishes, hopes, past hurts, and disappointments can lead . . . to . . . errors" (Goldenthal, 2005, p. 23) both in individual and family therapy. Within this discovery, Böszörményi-Nagy, a trained psychoanalyst, contributed a great deal to the contextual model by the incorporation of elements of the psychoanalytic theories with the systemic theories, recognizing the influence of one family member on family development. It is important to emphasize that according to the contextual model, individual factors are always looked at in the relational context because "to be is to be relational" (Lothstein, 1996, cited by Gangamma, 2008, p. 11). This contribution has practical application in therapy in forms of acknowledgment and assessment of individual psychological differences.

Transactions

The third dimension of contextual theory, transactions, indicates that the interactional patterns in families are mutual. Although both contextual and systemic approaches agree on the circular nature of relationships, the contextual model sees families as dynamic self-regulatory systems (Whitchurch & Constantine, 1993, cited by Gangamma, p. 12) in the state of permanent instability of structure, roles, and communication patterns, functioning to either create relational change or to preserve the current situation. According to contextual theory, people strive for identity and clear boundaries, and our identities only exist in comparison to others. As social beings we need complementarity in meaningful relationships in the family, when "the other would no longer be seen as superior or inferior . . . ," which produces ". . . a less rigid form of identity with which we make contrast between 'us' and 'them' " (Chaplin, 2008, p. 25). In this context a healthy family fulfills the goals and needs of both the individual and the family.

Relational Ethics

Probably the most significant contribution of the contextual model is the development of its groundbreaking fourth dimension, the concept of relational ethics. It is based on a strong belief that our evolution, health, and even survival depend on the quality of human relationships. In this context relational ethics consider reciprocal trust, loyalty, and genuineness to be the key conditions of strong relationships in families.

Contextual family therapy was one of the first theories recognizing that family therapy and moral questions are inseparable and that the ethical aspects of family relationships and therapy are highly interconnected

(Fowers &Wagner, 1997). This can be an important concept in working with Muslim families since Islam as a religion has a strong emphasis on morality in human interactions. Thus, family members can easily relate to this moral aspect of human relationships and hold themselves accountable for their unjust and unfair behavior.

The word 'context' has important meaning within the contextual model in general and in relational ethics in particular. 'Context' signifies that clients are dynamically attached to their long-term relational and multigenerational roots. It refers to a network of contacts, built in the process of giving and receiving, and their interdependence with each other, which makes sense within the collectivistic cultural backgrounds of Muslim families.

Relational ethics using a multigenerational perspective focuses on both between and within generational functions and roles of loyalty to family and society, fairness, accountability, trustworthiness, and reciprocity. Developing from basic needs and individual experiences, relational ethics are more than a code of socially accepted behaviors. In all its intricacy mankind can be justifiably seen as either essentially selfish, as altruistic and good-natured, or as morally ambivalent. However, "our evolutionary inheritance" shows that "we are moral beings to the core" (de Waal, cited by Labanyi, 2009, p. 21). Therefore, relational ethics is naturally present in individuals, families, and broader society and can be greatly emphasized in working with Muslim families.

It is important to note that all family interactions are acts of giving and receiving. Each act brings a new balance or imbalance to the ledgers of entitlement and indebtedness. Because the contextual model defines trustworthy relationships as mature and without using exploitation, a ledger is balanced when all family members take responsibility for making a sincere effort to consider each other's welfare, rather than make a contribution of 'equal value.'

Developing from the metaphor of a ledger, the concept of entitlement relates to family members' ability to prioritize other's needs, welfare, and interests over their own. In a fair exchange of give and take a constructive entitlement is earned, and each person who cares about another family member becomes entitled to receive love and care. Those who are subjected to unjust factual realities and are treated unfairly, however, obtain destructive entitlements and are more likely to compensate by treating others unfairly.

Although both experiences are important, compensations for destructive entitlements spanning through generations are spoken about more often, and families bring them to family therapy more than any other issues. Böszörményi-Nagy believed that his model applied to all relationships, including society as a whole, and that all relational conflicts are results of destructive entitlements, whether an ethnic war in Syria, conflicts in Afghanistan, substance abuse on the street corner, or unhappy adult children in your house. In another words, this model offers a logical explanation as to why some individuals are "predisposed to engage in repetitive and harmful behaviors that often affect those that did not victimize them and therefore are innocent" (Böszörményi-Nagy & Krasner, 1986, cited by Gangamma, 2008, p. 2).

Although, as any other theory, contextual family therapy has both its strengths and limitations, the contributions of Böszörményi-Nagy to its development can hardly be exaggerated. He was probably the first to recognize the inseparability of the behavioral and ethical dimensions and believed the ethical dimension was an important and integral part of many models for family and individual therapy. Perhaps because of this discovery, this model seems to identify the nature of family relationships in all their complexity, including the multigenerational dynamic, "better than any other major family therapy approaches" (Fowers & Wagner, 1997). Many of the Muslim families therapists work with come from a multicultural and multi-ethnic family of origin and from countries with a long and dramatic history of social and ethnic conflicts. Therefore, the contextual model sheds a new light on the instabilities of family and individual goals, 'split loyalties' and legacies of 'created realities,' handed down through generations.

Integrating the importance of the individual within the systemic model and the multigenerational perspective, contextual theory offers a distinctive rationalization for the disturbing phenomena of the intergenerational transmission of violence (both in family and broader societal contexts) using the main concepts of trust, loyalty, justice, and entitlement.

Contextual Therapy Concepts

Multidirected Partiality

Multidirected partiality is one of the main contextual therapy concepts (Böszörményi-Nagy & Krasner, 1986). The therapist must recognize the different perspectives of all family members in therapy in addition to understanding the other systems with which they are involved. The task can be accomplished by sympathizing with each individual in the family and acknowledging his or her contributions towards greater good for the whole family (Böszörményi-Nagy & Krasner, 1986). The therapist must acknowledge past injustices and promote fairness in the family for each person by aligning with different members of the family at different times to establish justice and fairness. In some situations, the therapist supports a family member who seems to be the most vulnerable. Multidirected partiality helps the therapist validate, empathize, understand, and acknowledge family members' contributions and also hold them responsible for the influences their behavior has on others. This task is difficult to accomplish when the person who is responsible for the injustice is in therapy and has a close relationship with all family members. Thus, in some situations, individual sessions may help with the examinations of past injustices before family members can safely examine those issues together. The most important aspect of multidirected partiality is to assess the impact of mediations in helping family members heal by discussing relational injustices with all family members present in sessions.

Relational Ethics

As discussed before, the "balance of equitable fairness between people" is called relational ethics (Böszörményi-Nagy & Ulrich, 1981, p. 160). The main focus of a contextual therapist is helping families use their relational resources equally and "balance the ledger." This can be accomplished by making all family members take responsibility for their parts in family relational dynamics. If the family environment is healthy and trustworthy, all family members, then, are obligated and have responsibility to give back to their family (Böszörményi-Nagy & Spark, 1973).

Children have a special place with the context of family relationships because they have limited resources in terms of their family contributions but have rights as members of a family. Parents should be the most reliable source of support for their children and should give their children all the resources their parents gave them (Böszörményi-Nagy & Krasner, 1986). Once children are older, they will start contributing to the family, and ultimately by caring for their elderly parents or their own children they rebalance the family scales. The cycle of relational ethic is interesting in being a circular process of giving but not expecting to receive and nevertheless receiving because of being giving. Over several generations, this process of giving and receiving becomes balanced, and the family will continue to prosper. Relational ethics are easier to discuss and process with Muslim families since honoring relational ethics is an inherent part of the collectivistic cultural context and expectations in Eastern societies.

Entitlement

Individuals who are dependable, fair minded, and care about the well-being of others and are good at acknowledging what others have given them earn constructive entitlement or merit in relationships. In many situations, though, individuals may feel that they were certainly not given what they deserved. They may feel that their needs were not met or that they were mistreated or abused, particularly during their childhoods. Therefore, they may seek what they think they deserve from those who were not even in control of providing the care for them or hurting them. In most situations, these past experiences of being treated unfairly have made them clueless about the distress of others, which has been referred to as constructive entitlement (Böszörményi-Nagy & Krasner, 1986).

Parentification is often one of the most serious consequences of destructive entitlement. This typically comprises unbalanced hierarchical boundaries, like having a child be responsible for the care and well-being of a parent (Böszörményi-Nagy & Ulrich, 1981). Parentification creates an unbalanced and reversed cycle of reciprocity between a parent and child. The child who is supposed to receive care from his or her parents does not receive it and seeks restoration from the next generation. The same pattern of parentification happens between marital partners when one partner has to 'parent' and take care of the other with no reciprocity.

The good news is that destructive entitlement can be eliminated by going through the exoneration process, which means the individual comprehends the reason for not receiving the care she/he deserved from the perspective of the person who did not provide the care (Böszörményi-Nagy & Krasner, 1986). In this process, the individual simply reassesses and reevaluates the blamed person's personal and relational assets, competencies, strengths, limitations, choices, and own victimization. This process will help the person with destructive entitlement understand

and empathize with the blamed person. Once this task is accomplished, the therapist can help the destructively entitled individual to understand his/her process of victimizing others. This can eventually help the person work on examining his or her own behavior and earn constructive entitlement.

The process of exoneration is more about understanding the other person's context, which in no way frees the blamed person from taking responsibility for his or her behavior. Individuals have to be accountable for the agony and damage they have caused for others. However, the exoneration process allows the victimized person to gain a sense of power by acknowledging his or her own victimization while understanding the blamed person's contextual resources. Once individuals accept that their victimization was not their fault, they feel less guilty and shift the responsibility to the offender. At the same time, victims can work on their own destructive entitlement and changing their own behaviors. Therefore, exoneration is the process of understanding victimization and powerlessness and acknowledging the responsibility of the offender for the abuse of power in the relationship. From this systemic perspective, victims can understand how they use their victimization to abuse others and continue the vicious cycle of destructive entitlement.

Loyalty

Loyalty is having commitment and strong connections to people who deserve entitlement (Böszörményi-Nagy & Krasner, 1986). People have loyalty conflicts or develop split loyalties when they are forced to divide their allegiances between two groups or individuals who oppose each other, such as being loyal to their family of origin but also wanting to be loyal to their family of procreation, or being loyal to one's mother, who expects the child not to have the same level of loyalty to the father. Relational ethics require the individual with the split loyalty towards different relational systems to balance these relationships, but often individuals do not have the proper resources to undertake this very difficult task.

According to Böszörményi-Nagy and Krasner (1986), invisible loyalty is about having a sense of ambivalence or avoidance about loyalty to others. This happens when an individual feels obligated to a parent or a spouse but is ambivalent about the obligation or does not admit to the impact of that loyalty on current issues and circumstances. It is often the case that invisible loyalties prevent individuals from truly committing to other relationships that deserve loyalty and balance. This concept has a lot of applicability for Muslim families due to multilayered and complex relational loyalties to the family of origin, which are inherently very strong in Eastern cultures, and very often prevents individuals from developing healthy loyalties to their family of procreation. A frank and candid conversation about the healthy balance individuals need to achieve can be very helpful for Muslim families dealing with the invisible loyalties they may have towards their parents versus their spouses.

Legacy

Legacy is when the current generation takes care of their ethical obligations by working on their relational conflicts to help their future generation get along better. In reality, legacies are "the relational roots of transgenerational consequences" (Böszörményi-Nagy & Krasner, 1986, p. 131). It is this wisdom about justice, fairness, reciprocal caring, and entitlement that families can pass from one generation to another as their legacy. This concept can also be easily conceptualized and discussed with Muslim families due to their collectivistic cultural background and the importance of the concept of legacy as part of their ethical obligations towards the previous and also next generation.

Case Example

Asma, a 54-year-old Afghani woman, came to see me because of her ambivalence about divorcing her husband. They had been married for 34 years and separated for approximately five months. Asma and her husband had three adult children, and she had recently started working in a daycare after being a full-time homemaker for many years.

Asma talked about the long-term physical and verbal abuse by her husband throughout her marriage that at times was "unbearable." However, she saw her role as a wife and a mother as more central and tried her best to explain her husband's behavior as an indication of his own abuse issues in his family of origin. I tried to have deeper-level conversations about her role as a wife and a mother within her Eastern cultural context and how her own needs were sacrificed in this process. Asma cried when I empathized about how difficult and unfair it had been for her and how she had not even given herself permission to feel bad about her position in relation to others. We explored Asma's parents' relationship. She stated that her father was also abusive towards her mother and that her mother became very depressed and at times almost nonfunctioning. Over the first few conversations, I realized that Asma was a parentified child in her family of origin and had to care for her mother and siblings as the oldest child. I used the entitlement framework to explore the gender-based legacies of being a woman and how her needs were not met. She had many stories about ways that she had taken care of others without anyone caring about her needs. We talked about how both in her marriage and her family of origin, her 'ledger' was so unfairly balanced. We also processed the impact of gender and the further marginalization of her needs in society and the social messages about women's loyalty and duty to stay married. Together, we explored the 'roots' of these loyalty patterns, connecting it to all the messages she had received in her family of origin and society about women. These interventions helped her explore her family of origin's relational ethics and her current marital relationship and also guided her towards exoneration by broadening the scope of what she was feeling guilty about and placing her behavior in a broader context.

I helped Asma appreciate her own sense of agency in initiating a separation from her husband and finding a job at her age after all these years of being a wife and a mother. I used multidirected partiality to help Asma make her own decision about divorcing her husband but also think about the consequences of her decision for everyone in the family. However, when she discussed the impact of her divorce on her adult children and her husband, she was encouraged to not get 'trapped' into putting their needs before her own again. At first, she was thinking that the divorce might make her husband even angrier at her because she would not be there to take care of him. However, she also talked about how continuing the relationship would not be a viable option either. She came to the realization that she also deserved to have a peaceful life after all the years of taking care of others. However, since she had never been able to communicate her feelings openly and honestly with her husband, Salim, I suggested that she should invite her husband to seek relational therapy, and to her surprise he agreed to come to therapy. Asma spent some time discussing her pain in relation to how she had been treated over the years, and Salim was challenged to listen to her story and validate her perspective. When given a chance, Salim also discussed his family of origin and his conflictual relationship with his mother because he felt that she never protected him from his abusive father. Therefore, I was able to challenge both of them to understand the impact of these factual problems, which stemmed from their families of origin but had never been processed and resolved. At the end, she decided to remain separated until they could renegotiate a better level of understanding about their relational issues and find a way to either resolve or forgive. It seems like integrating a focus on gender and power with the constructs of legacies, entitlement, relational ethics, and loyalty helped Asma be able to make a conscious and informed decision about her marital relationship and also challenged Salim to recognize the legacies of his own relational issues and his invisible loyalties to his family of origin.

Summary

Contextual family therapy's biggest contribution to the family therapy field is filling a gap with respect to relational justice in families. Even though there are many family therapy theories that have examined the constructs of family structure, transgenerational patterns, and interactions, contextual family therapy is the only theory that has examined the constructs of loyalty, posterity, fairness, and relational ethics (Goldenthal, 1996). Contextual family therapy was not intended to be a new family therapy model but aimed to integrate the important principles of other psychotherapy models and add constructs related to relational justice (Böszörményi-Nagy & Krasner, 1986). Perhaps this model is not as theoretical as it is socioethical (Goldenthal, 1996; Grunebaum, 1987). It is a framework or set of ideas that offers the use of many techniques to help people increase their capability for attaining greater balance in their familial relationships.

Contextual family therapy encourages a shift in family members' intentions towards truthfulness, honesty, justice, and relational integrity for all family members and other systems they are part of. Contextual family therapy's main goal is to increase relational resources for families and enhance healthy development and growth for both the current family and future generations. If families experience their relationships as fair and balanced, individuals feel good about giving to others and also ask others to meet their needs in open conversations with each other.

Contextual therapy's focus is on people's resources more than on their pathology, which makes it a powerful model to use when working with Muslim families.

REFERENCES

Böszörményi-Nagy, I., & Krasner, B.R. (1986). *Between give and take*. New York: Brunner/Mazel Publications.

Böszörményi-Nagy, I., & Spark, G. (1973). *Invisible loyalties*. New York: Harper & Row Publications.

Böszörményi-Nagy, I., & Ulrich, D.N. (1981). Contextual family therapy. In A.S. Gurman, & D.P. Kniskern (Eds.), *Handbook of family therapy*. New York: Brunner & Mazel Publications.

Carey, B. (2007, February 13). Ivan Böszörményi-Nagy, 86, an innovator of family therapy. *The New York Times*. Retrieved from http://query.nytimes.com/gst/fullpage.html?res=9C07E4D81F3FF930A25751C0A9619C8B63

Chaplin, J. (2008). *Deep equality: Living in the flow of natural rhythms*. Saint Austell, United Kingdom: John Hunt Publishing.

Fowers, B.J., & Wagner, A. (1997). Are trustworthiness and fairness enough? Contextual family therapy and the good family. *Journal of Marital and Family Therapy, 23*, Retrieved from http://findarticles.com/p/articles/mi_qa3658/is_199704/ai_n8776815/

Gangamma, R. (2008). *Relational ethics among couples in therapy*. Doctoral dissertation presented in partial fulfillment of the requirements for the degree, Ohio State University. Retrieved from http://etd.ohiolink.edu/send-pdf.cgi/Gangamma%20Rashmi.pdf?osu1222191012

Goldenthal, P. (1996). *Doing contextual therapy*. New York: W.W. Norton.

Goldenthal, P. (2005). *Helping children and families: A new treatment model integrating psychodynamic, behavioral, and contextual approaches*. Hoboken, New Jersey: John Wiley & Sons.

Grunebaum, J. (1987). Multidirected partiality and the "parental imperative". *Psychotherapy, 24*, 646–656.

Krasner, B.R., & Joyce, A.J. (1995). *Truth, trust and relationships: Healing interventions in contextual therapy*. London: Routledge Publications.

Labanyi, P. (2009). Rediscovering what really matters. Judgment, authenticity and the moral code of psychotherapy, eisteach. *Quarterly Journal of Counseling and Psychotherapy, 9* (2).

Piercy, F.P., Sprenkle, D.H., & Wetchler, J.L. (1996). *Family therapy sourcebook*. New York: Guilford Press.

Shpungina, E. (2009). *Jews in Latvia*. Latvia: Latvian Council of Jewish Communities.

CHAPTER 11

FEMINIST FAMILY THERAPY

"Personal is political" is the main framework of the feminist perspective, indicating that women's personal experiences cannot be separated from their sociopolitical conditions, contextual factors, and everyday realities. Feminist family therapy's emphasis is on empowering women in families in order to change women's conventional positions that obstruct their progress and growth. Feminist therapy was influenced by the women's movement in the late 1960s in the US and other Western countries. However, an authentic and grassroots movement has grown in Muslim countries and has been helping women redefine themselves in family relationships (Daneshpour, 2009). Overall, feminist therapy's main emphasis is on supporting women to have higher level of confidence, learn to communicate their needs better, understand their relational dynamics, and learn to respect themselves while staying connected with family members. This approach is very useful in working with Muslim families because of the way it defines gender dynamics and challenges traditional family relationships. Feminist therapists advocate for the development of equal and reciprocal relationships in families. The therapist must believe that the client is the expert and should be helped to develop the needed skills to function independently to reach her own unique potential.

FEMINIST THERAPY

There is no one specific person who was the originator of feminist therapy. Feminists in the family therapy field are familiar with all other family therapy theories and have tried to keep useful elements of other theories in working with families while eliminating the sexist qualities of these theories. Therefore, feminist therapy's main goal is to empower women to pay attention to gender dynamics in families rather than adjusting to existing social roles and to realize the impact of socialization as the major sources or even the cause of many relational issues in any society. Feminist therapy's fundamental concept is honoring equality in all relationships, including professional relationships. Therefore, the therapist offers assistance and possibly some knowledge about the impact of gender and power on relational problems, but ultimately the clients need to make a decision about what would be a desired outcome for themselves and for their lives. This framework uses personal power as the main source for changing relational dynamics. Feminist therapists are encouraged to assist both men and women to discover and recognize the roots of their relational problems and discontent and find ways to deal with the influences of gender power in their relationships.

Feminist therapy can be extremely valuable for both men and women. Men are greatly influenced by gender role constrictions like demands for strength, autonomous decision-making, and competition and can be helped to relieve themselves from these restrictions through this therapeutic process. Men in traditional societies like Middle Eastern and other Eastern countries are especially influenced by these restrictions and can greatly benefit from feminist family therapy. Men also have to deal with societal influences with regards to not expressing vulnerability, sensitivity, and empathy. Men and women are both subjugated to our patriarchal societies' rules, cultural norms, and gender stereotypes. Feminist therapy can help men work through many of these issues and learn new skills to explore matters related to feelings, self-disclosure, intimacy, and vulnerability.

Feminist philosophies are based on four different frameworks—socialist, radical, cultural, and liberal—each achieving different therapeutic goals. Feminists with a socialist perspective see a great need for change in all institutional and social relationships and believe that these institutions are perpetuating a vicious cycle of gender inequality. Feminists with a radical perspective are advocating for change in all gender relations and societal institutions and attempt to increase women's awareness of sexual politics, relationships with men, and aspirations and attitudes about having children. Feminists with a cultural perspective advocate for cultural transformation and state that women are not valued in societies, which greatly impacts women's sense of self in many important ways. Feminists with a liberal perspective emphasize the challenges women face with regards to self-awareness, self-respect, self-esteem, and egalitarianism in all relationships. It is obvious that there are many commonalities in these perspectives, and all are integrated around the idea of equality.

Feminist therapy is also unique in regards to dealing with four major approaches to therapy. These are consciousness-raising, analysis of gender role, resocialization, and social activism. Consciousness-raising is an approach that can be used with small leaderless groups to discuss women's unique and collective experiences. These group discussions can help women realize that other women may have the same experiences and that listening and supporting each other can empower all of them. Examining the impact of oppression and patriarchal socialization on personal stress and finding solutions can be empowering and liberating for women. Participating in social actions and making grassroots changes are only possible when women are culturally and socially aware and feel empowered to move towards eliminating oppression.

Analyzing gender role socialization is about paying closer attention to the client's emotional and mental stress and coping skills. Based on this approach, clients are helped to understand the influences of cultural and social norms and expectations on their own functioning, which, in turn, helps them become more aware of gender role norms (Dankoski, Penn, Carlson, & Hecker, 1998). Once the client becomes more conscious about the implicit and explicit impact of gender socialization, it becomes possible to explore the origins of the client's emotional and mental stress. Only then can the client gain knowledge about her own socialization pattern and go through the process of change.

Resocialization can happen only after clients have consciously understood the influences of the patterns of social and gender roles and requires understanding the client's belief system. Once clients develop new ideas about the influences of gender dynamics, they view relationships differently and may develop new coping skills. Clients can also learn new techniques to help them develop higher self-esteem, become more assertive, and have better self-perception. Resocialization's main goal is to help clients increase their emotional well-being.

Social activism is somewhat more political, and therapists may have a hard time using it in their practice. It is embedded in the notion that "personal is political" and that clients' problems are related to the societal and political atmosphere. In this approach, both therapist and client must get involved as social activists and fight for societal and political change. Clients can be encouraged to speak out or even organize rallies and write letters to authorities. Feminist therapists advocate for social change as a crucial aspect of improving the emotional and mental health of all individuals, including men and women in families.

Corey (2001) discusses five interconnected principles for feminist therapy: 1) The personal is political, and change in societal dynamics happens only when we take this issue seriously. 2) Therapist and client have equal power in the therapeutic relationship. The client is in charge of any changes and defines the relationship dynamics, and the therapist provides new knowledge, insight, and information. 3) Women's life experiences are as important as men's experiences and need to be respected. 4) Stress and mental illness need to be redefined and reformulated and should include internal as well as external reasons for stress. Resistance and pain reveal a positive proof for the need to live and overcome stress and are not a sign of weakness. 5) Feminist perspectives comprehensively examine subjugation and repression of both men and women and believe that these repressive experiences have an overwhelming impact on their beliefs and perceptions.

According to Walker (1990), feminist therapy teaches women to gain and use power in relationships. It also teaches them to work on enhancing their own strengths because many traditional therapeutic models focus on a woman's inadequacies and limitations. Feminist therapists hope that women search for their own strengths, rely on their own potentials, and try to utilize them effectively. Feminist family therapy does not use psychopathology to label women and their relationships and rejects the medical model. Women's emotional and relational problems are understood and evaluated based on their social context and as a way to cope with their personal and relational difficulties. Using this model, women are taught to recognize their cognitive abilities and are encouraged to educate themselves. They are also taught to learn to accept and validate each other's emotional reactions in different situations. Self-disclosure is highly valued and viewed as a powerful way to emotionally connect the therapist and clients together and enhance their therapeutic relationships.

Feminist therapy is constructive and valuable in any society for both women and men mainly because, first, the goal is not just changing relational dynamics and personal viewpoint but changing traditional societal views of these relationships. Second, understanding the impact of gender dynamics and how it can cause emotional distress and undesirable behavior can be very beneficial to both men and women. Finally, feminist therapy helps both men and women understand the influences of their socialization as well as internal, external, and contextual forces that impact their identities and their relational difficulties.

Moreover, men and masculine patterns of thoughts and behavior have dominated women's lives across the globe. Until very recently, studies of human behavior and psychological patterns of emotional relationships have often been conducted by men on men but were indiscriminately and equally applied to women. The outcomes of these studies are not useful because men and women do not have the same opportunities, do not emotionally develop the same way due to environmental influences, and do not view the world the same based on the different messages they receive. One of the main influences is social media, which gives young children strong messages about how they should behave based on their gender. Boys are portrayed as being dominant, aggressive, autonomous, self-reliant, and successful while girls are portrayed as being submissive, docile, emotional, sweet, well behaved, and beautiful. However, girls receive a paradoxical message since the same attributes that are proper and acceptable for young girls are not proper and suitable for grown women. In addition, men's view of the world is more based on power and competition, whereas women's view of the world is more through the lens of relationships and connections to others. Therefore, assumptions about men's behavior are not a very good representation of women's behavior.

Women have been socialized to be caring and nurturing even though these traits don't bring much power for women. They are not valued, and their needs are not as important as men in any society, including Muslim societies. These social norms make women powerless in their interactions with others even though these characteristics are not inherently negative. Ideally both men and women should be commended for all the roles they play. However, society does not value women's parenting and child-rearing skills as much as career skills. Men are influenced by these social norms as well because men are not valued for staying home to raise children and taking care of household needs either.

Feminist therapists understand the impact of these issues on family relationships and acknowledge how much connections and care are important in individuals' lives. They consider societal bias in terms of gender role expectations in male-dominated societies and respect the experiences of women and their feelings as acceptable and important. Feminist therapists focus on issues related to family and marital relationships; choices for the timing of having children; balancing family life and career opportunities; emotional, sexual, and physical abuse; and body image issues, confidence, and self-esteem. Additionally, empowering women in today's world is an important part of feminist therapy. These interests are based on a gender-balanced system for therapy. Feminist therapy can be integrated and used in conjunction with other models in order to enrich and enlighten both men's and women's lives.

Feminist therapy has been criticized because some therapists have taken the model too far. Some feminist therapists have expected women to handle their relational difficulties the 'right' way, which has been the therapist's way, and have persuaded women to act or to look at things differently when they have not wanted to do that. An impartial and unbiased therapist should only offer encouragement and knowledge and challenge the client to assess her own life circumstances and make her own decisions. Furthermore, feminist therapy may have some biases and not be neutral. They advocate for a definite change at the societal level, but they have to be careful not to force their views on clients. Clients need to take responsibility for their own behaviors and interactions and realize that even though society and gender role expectations impact their relational dynamics, they can change these patterns.

In conclusion, feminist therapy should be viewed at an essential therapeutic framework in any society today. The same way that human beings continue to make progress in understanding our psychological needs, we have to come up with new models to meet the needs of our societies. Feminist therapists have shown commitment in dismantling the dysfunctional power hierarchy for both men and women by using therapeutic approaches and interventions that intend to empower clients and create societal change and transformation. A case example will highlight how this model can be used with Muslim couples.

Case Example

Maha (35) and Hamid (39), an Iraqi couple, came to see me when their second child was about nine months old. Maha was having a hard time being at home with two kids and not receiving much support from Hamid. She had been working before the birth of their second child, but quit her job, and Hamid became the sole provider and was very stressed about their current situation and their finances. Hamid claimed that he had the desire to be more involved as a father but did not know how to balance all his responsibilities outside their home and also be an active father. It was obvious that both felt overwhelmed and unappreciated by their partners even though they were both greatly contributing to their family's well-being. I tried to acknowledge their difficult situation and encouraged them to recognize each other's contributions as well. However, Hamid was greatly struggling to recognize Maha's contribution to their family's well-being at the same level as his contribution and was using his paycheck as a solid proof of his contribution. I listed the number of tasks Maha was performing and challenged Hamid to value Maha's household contributions to help the family function. I encouraged Maha to write down every task she performed at home for two days to help Hamid understand the amount of work she needed to do to take care of all the chores at their home. This intervention helped Hamid realize how much Maha was contributing to the family.

Using a genogram I searched for ways the couple's expectations about marriage and parenting had been shaped by the legacy of gender socialization messages they had received about their parents' contribution to family life. Hamid's and Maha's mothers both were housewives, and their fathers were the only breadwinners. We discussed how the legacy of these unconscious expectations of marital roles had impacted their expectations of their own roles. We also discussed their parents' traditional social context and their limited choices, which were very different than Maha and Hamid's current social context. I also challenged Hamid and Maha to talk about the details of both their mothers' and fathers' contributions to family life. It was interesting that they both had a hard time thinking about their mothers' contributions to family functioning, so I confronted them to think about ways both of their families had taken their mothers for granted.

As we explored Hamid and Maha's gendered expectations in their families of origin, Hamid talked about how he could easily recognize his father's hard work and his financial contributions to the family, but he also remembered him as an uninvolved father who was very detached from Hamid and his siblings. Therefore, I suggested that he may want to talk to his father about how he felt about their detached relationship. Even though Hamid was apprehensive about having the conversation with his father, and took a while to connect with his father, the conversation went very well. Hamid's father talked about his regret that his long working hours had not allowed him to spend more time with his children, which helped Hamid understand that his father had to focus on being a provider and did not intend to be detached from the family. I also encouraged Hamid to talk to his mother about her contribution to the family and let her know that he appreciated what she has done for him while he was growing up. These conversations helped Hamid and his father start spending more time together, and in turn Hamid realized his own distanced relationship from his two young children. He talked about wanting to be more emotionally connected to his children and needing to know how he could learn to balance his obligations to work and family.

Maha needed several sessions to process her own emotional reactions to her mother's role as a homemaker. She talked about how she liked having her mother at home when she was growing up but also resented the fact that her mother did not do anything more than be a full-time homemaker and was not a better role model for her daughters. Together, we explored her mother's social context and her real options in a very traditional society where men and women got married and men became sole providers and women became homemakers. Maha was able to differentiate between her mother's past social context and her own with regards to the meaning of motherhood and realized that her options and the higher level of support she received from her husband were not even comparable to her mother's. I encouraged Maha to talk to her parents, who lived in Iraq, about the challenges they had to work through to provide for the family. Maha also processed these issues with her sister. Later on, Maha and I discussed her struggles to balance work and family, and she disclosed that she was worried she had lost her sense of independence by quitting her job. Feminist theory informs us that women in all societies have a tendency to place the needs of others first, so I challenged Maha to think about her own needs for self-fulfillment. Maha was very articulate about her desire to not rely on the children for self-fulfillment the same way her mother may have done and began searching for ways to assert her own sense of identity. I also had to explain to Hamid how Maha's need for self-fulfillment would help their marital relationship and asked him to listen and respond to this new assertiveness that Maha showed. Like many women I have worked with throughout the years, Maha also struggled with balancing being a full-time mother and homemaker and not neglecting her own needs at the same time. She finally decided to take a course at the local university to work towards advancing her education but also started to reframe the decisions she made about parenting as a needed priority and not as a forced obligation. In this way, Maha was able to be emotionally available and care for her children without seeing them as the only source of her well-being.

As we continued our therapeutic work together, I started noticing the couple's very implicit power imbalances and encouraged them to openly talk about how they perceived fairness and justice in their relationship. I used my feminist lens to discuss the importance of equal involvement in childcare and encouraged Hamid to participate more fairly in caring for the children when he was at home. Further, we processed Maha's desire for self-fulfillment and how Hamid wanted to respond to Maha's needs with respect. I tried to help them process the impact of these changes for their children's emotional and relational health, and both agreed that Hamid's greater parental involvement and Maha's greater sense of self-fulfillment would be greatly beneficial to their children's well-being. Hamid started to take care of their children in the evenings that Maha was taking a class. Both Maha and Hamid felt that this plan balanced their parental obligations to their children better and gave them personal freedom at the same time that they fulfilled their sense of accountability towards their family. The focus on using a feminist therapy perspective in balancing their gender socialization and power dynamics helped this couple reorganize their relationship into a more egalitarian relationship that was less controlled by unconscious, gendered, and family of origin legacies.

Summary

Knudson-Martin (1997) writes: "Just as one cannot not communicate, one also cannot not do gender, [and] therapists who accept this premise . . . find themselves in the position of having no choice but to think about and respond to clinical problems in relation to gender. The question is not whether to address gender, but how" (p. 429).

If we review all the definitions of feminist family therapy, the most salient definition is how the therapist is an agent for social change (Daneshpour, 2009). Feminism as it relates to therapy can be defined as an approach with the themes of a nonhierarchical relationship negotiated between men and women; the willingness of partners to discuss specific gender role patterns that work for them; and allowing women to make personal and professional decisions within the context of a committed relationship (Whipple, 1996). Feminist family therapy is an approach that perceives sexism and patriarchy as the root of relational imbalances within the historical and social contexts of all societies.

Feminist family therapists working with Muslim couples should challenge the politics of gender and power in all the relationships that clients are surrounded by in their families, communities, and societies. However, family therapists have to be careful not to assume that Muslim couples are the only group that may have difficulty with their gender-imbalanced relationships. Feminist movements began in Western countries because of the oppressive patriarchal gender dynamics existing in families and in all social and economic contexts. Therefore, it is necessary to view patriarchy as a problem impacting all men and women in the context of all societies and all families, including Muslim families.

References

Corey, G. (2001). *Theory and practice of counseling and psychotherapy* (6th ed., pp. 341–375). Wadsworth: Brooks Cole/Thompson Learning.

Daneshpour, M. (2009). Steadying the tectonic plates: On being Muslim, feminist academic, and family therapist. In K. Allen, A. Few, & S. Lloyd (Eds.), *Handbook of feminist family studies* (pp. 340-351). Thousand Oaks, CA: Sage Publications.

Dankoski, M.E., Penn, C.D., Carlson, T.D., & Hecker, L.L. (1998). What's in a name? A study of family therapists use and acceptance of the feminist perspective. *American Journal of Family Therapy, 26*, 95–104.

Knudson-Martin, C. (1997). The politics of gender in family therapy. *Journal of Marital and Family Therapy, 23*, 421–437.

Walker, L.E. (1990). A feminist therapist views the case. In D.W. Cantor (Ed.), *Women as therapists* (pp. 78-79). New York: Spring Publishing Company.

Whipple, V. (1996). Developing an identity as a feminist family therapist: Implications for training. *Journal of Marital Therapy, 22*, 381–396.

CHAPTER 12

POST-MODERN FAMILY THERAPY

The term 'post-modernism' has been used in contemporary and academic circles across many different cultures. This is a historical period marked by transition and new ways of seeing the world called the post-modern era. In its simplest form, the transition from the modern to the post-modern era is marked by societal belief that there is no objective, absolute, and fixed reality for all people and that there are many equally valid ways that the world can be viewed and people can behave (Anderson, 1990). Furthermore, the post-modernist perspective reveals that societies should not operate based on static principles that have traditionally made a division between right and wrong, proper and improper, and virtuous and vicious. For an increasing number of people, a family's ideal principles are not as much embedded in sacrosanct doctrines of organized religion and civic society. They are more or less a very sequestered synthesis of personal, intimate, and contextual principles. This approach is useful in working with Muslim families because it challenges the notion of objective reality and knowledge and invites therapists to be curious about the meaning behind human interactions without assigning judgment and blame. In order to have a better appreciation for this model, it is essential to evaluate several concepts that have helped the formation of this approach in family therapy.

MODERNISM AND POST-MODERNISM

Modernism defines an interesting period from the late nineteenth to the mid-twentieth century when many fundamental changes happened in

European culture. This period was marked by a strong belief in reason and freedom, and progress and growth became the philosophy of the enlightenment. A primary principle in this period was the progression in analyzing the fundamental construction of both the arts and the sciences. Some believe that post-modernism does not represent a different era (Mills & Sprenkle, 1995). It basically represents how modernism had existed long enough to reflect on itself and criticize aspects of modernism that were no longer working. Others claim that the fundamental difference between modernism and post-modernism is that post-modernists are not nostalgic and do not reminisce about the past. Still others assert that we cannot think of post-modernism as a distinct chronological era, but rather a distinct intellectual paradigm shift with regards to theoretical views, arts, architecture, and even contemplating what it means to be human. Thus, it seems like the main difference between modernism and post-modernism is the way they see the usefulness of enlightenment, belief in human progress, science, and reason, for social and cultural understandings.

Family therapy, like all other psychological models, first developed during the modernism era and integrated all its assumptions. However, since first- and second-order therapy were already part of family therapists' conceptualization, they became familiarized with modernism after post-modernism (Anderson, 1997).

Family Therapy and Post-Modernism

Family therapy, which adapted general system theory as its main framework, was the most distinctive form of practice and major paradigm that was used in working with families in the 1980s. This kind of family therapy, in which the therapist observes the family systems dynamics and is very careful not to become part of the family system, is first-order family therapy. Second-order family therapy relied on the concept of constructivism, which claims that our knowledge of the external world results from our instinctive and intrinsic mental and sensual structures (Maturana & Varela, 1984). This way of thinking is a major change from the previous stance of therapists claiming that external reality was knowable. Therefore, family therapists needed to incorporate their own subjective, personal, and theoretical predisposition as part of their observation and become more aware of their own perceptions.

Constructivism

The term 'constructivism,' which later was associated by family therapists with second-order cybernetics, was first promoted by cognitive psychologist Ernst von Glasersfeld (1984). He pulled together the philosophical traditions from Kant to Piaget, strengthened by the scientific advances in cybernetic biology and cognition. He presented a model based on the idea that we don't discover our reality but rather construct and invent it in response to the world around us (Hoffman, 1985). Ultimate or preferred reality based on this way of thinking is a highly personal matter.

This way of thinking gained popularity with family therapists in need of a conceptual framework strong enough to create stability when values were shifting in a post-modern world. The term 'constructivism' was used by many therapists who believed that people's personal beliefs about their life experiences and the meanings they assigned to those beliefs should have the highest priority in the therapeutic conversation. The metaphor of constructed reality became a powerful concept that even the most troublesome personal realities (e.g., painful marital conflict) could be open to a more viable personal reconstruction.

Furthermore, this post-modern environment in two ways has tremendously influenced the evolution of family therapy. First, families have been changing, partly due to the increased prevalence of divorce during the last 20 years in all cultural contexts, including Middle Eastern countries. Second, over the last decade, theories explaining how reality is processed, or how we come to know what we know, have captured the attention of family therapists and have given the field a rich metaphorical context for working with families in the post-modern era.

Social Constructionism

Another way of reflecting on people's reality is based on the concept of social constructionism, which indicates that we create our own reality using language in an ongoing and steady relational and interactional process. Discourses about our experiences in the world are not based on contemplation about reality. It is more or less a byproduct of our collective interchanges (Gergen, 1991). Social constructionism is connected to a philosophy of community connection. It treats reality as part of a group interaction and essentially questions the existence of an essential self apart from others (Hoffman, 1990). The strong connection between social constructionism and family therapy has given rise to its current popularity in the field.

Family therapists need to be attentive to how families make meaning and perceive their own experiences in order for this model to be used successfully. This movement from constructivism to social constructionism has proven to be more clinically useful in working with families than first-order change therapy (Gergen, 1991). Cybernetics and constructivism lost their appeal to many family therapist like Hoffman (1993), who stated: "Postmodernism, whatever that meant, was a small black cloud on the horizon for many of us systemic people for several years, then it burst with thunder storm force on the field of family therapy" (p. 83).

The Influence of Post-Modern Theory on Family Therapy

Anderson and Goolishian (1988, 1992) are two clinicians leading the field in using post-modern therapy. They view social constructionism as a model that has played a large part in the development of their theoretical thinking along with the philosophical culture of hermeneutics.

The structure of post-modern therapy is less about techniques or different therapy phases. It focuses more on creating a safe environment for family members to have a meaningful conversation. This therapy process is characterized by an insightful and reflective stance on the part of the therapist. Questions focus on expanding and uncovering particular meanings for family members. Conversations revolve around clients knowing more about their lives, and the therapist avoids the invitation to get trapped into the position of being the one who has all the answers. The therapist may give some general advice or discuss research findings related to a specific problem and must be respectful of clients' reflections, beliefs, and reactions. The main impact of the therapeutic process in helping family members change should revolve around an open style of communication. When reflecting teams are used, team members have conversations with each other in front of the family about their observations of family members' interactions. The reflecting team, then, deliberates about their ideas based on what family members have discussed and enthusiastically respond to different kinds of meanings that develop throughout this process. After listening to the suggestions and ideas of the reflecting team, the family and therapist decide what to include, exclude, or use to develop these ideas in more details and collaborate on solutions generated from those conversations.

Structuralism and Post-Structuralism

Whenever we discuss modernism and post-modernism, a conversation about structuralism and post-structuralism will also become necessary. In essence structuralism is the notion that there are fixed relationship between different entities that go beyond time and often operate in opposition to each other. For example, Descartes discussed the structural opposition of our minds and bodies. Saussure discussed the semiotics of language and the inherent relationships between the structure of signs and signifiers. Freud discussed the mind's primary structure of conscious and unconscious, which are directly connected to our life and death instincts. Levi Strauss discussed the duality of cultures and myths, and Marx discussed dialectical materialism. All these concepts are stable at the system level and are observed by humans from outside the system.

Several fields confronted structuralism's capability in explaining these fixed and stable relationships between different entities. French philosopher Derrida challenged Saussure's (1959) semiotics assumption about words and their fixed meanings (Derrida, 1976). He claimed that understanding a text is not independent of understanding and contextualizing the authors' experiences because words are not "out there" to explain something that means the same thing to everyone regardless of their experiences. There are others who also challenged the structuralists' claim to an all-encompassing principle. For example, Einstein's theory of relativity challenged Newton's theory in physics, and French psychoanalyst Lacan challenged the structuralist works of Freud.

Structuralism had a fundamental impact on family therapy theories from general systems theory, which is based on the relationships between parts and the whole, and cybernetics, which views families as information-processing systems with feedback loops desiring homoeostasis at all costs, to the structural model, which views the family as a decision-making group, with generational boundaries and dynamic interactional patterns. These models were fundamental in determining and explaining families' interactional patterns. However, post-structuralism analysis percolated and challenged many assumptions of systemic therapy and its primary ideas and began to challenge the concept that there is only one single external reality. It seems like social constructionism was a major influence on systemic therapists and helped them a great deal in understanding the fluidity of language and meaning.

Language

Language is so crucial in the process of psychotherapy because of its static structure, which is supposed to represent reality. Language is also used to express our views, beliefs, and opinions. Therefore, we assume that when two people have a conversation with each other, they are able to share their thoughts in a way that the other person completely understands, and words are carefully associated with what they each understand them to mean. It seems impossible to understand, process, compare, and make sense of any discourse without taking the distinctive and historical rule of language into consideration (Lyotard, 1984). Lyotard states that we can only hope for a "little narrative" based on the personal and not the universal understanding of an absolute and objective truth. Gergen (1991) also confirms that understanding can only happen when people intimately interact with each other. Further, it is the meaning that people attach to their lives and how they express these meanings through language that facilitate client change. Therapy is aimed at "the form-giving, meaning-making part, the narrator who at every waking moment of our lives spins out its account of who we are and what we are doing and why we are doing it" (Anderson, 1990, p. 137).

It is crucial for therapists to explore the connection between understanding and language because the therapist uses language to uncover, rationalize, foresee, and influence change (Anderson, 1997). It is important to be sensitive in using this model when working with people from different cultures for whom English is not their first language. Muslim families, for example, may be perplexed by the 'non-expert' position of the post-modern therapist because Easterners prefer to listen to expert advice more than collaborate with the therapist about their issues. On the other hand, this is an important model in working with Muslim families because it gives families the freedom to express their feelings and explain their position on issues and be part of the decision-making process.

THE SELF

The contrast between the universal and the individual is one of the major themes of modernism. In Eastern cultures and religions, the construction of self is seen as an illusion, but Westerners view self within the context of an individualistic true self. The most fundamental aspect of psychoanalytic therapy is based on modernism and involves exploring layers of conscious and unconscious self to get into deeper aspects of an individual's psyche (Parry, 1991).

On the other hand, systemic family therapy viewed the family system as a whole and, instead of attending to the individual self, directed attention to the family system. Based on this perspective the corresponding concept of the psychodynamic 'true self' changed into the family system's attempt to self-correct itself. In this view, systemic family therapy changed the whole family and not just one individual. Broader influences of cultural contexts, institutional rules, and sociopolitical conditions and influences related to the independent individual's needs in the family were not equally considered or evaluated.

THERAPIST SELF-DISCLOSURE

Family therapists using post-modern approaches make less emphasis on hierarchy and first-order boundaries between therapist and client and may choose to share stories from their own lives when they feel they are relevant and appropriate to the therapeutic conversations. Self-disclosure has always been part of the experiential approaches such as those established by Whitaker & Bumberry (1988) and Satir (1964), but these second-order sensibilities have influenced even traditional family therapists towards a greater transparency.

Therapists who recognize their own bias and/or emotional reaction to clients' stories that correlates directly with clients' stories may openly share parts of these stories in an effort to clarify the personal roots of their position. When the therapist is no longer in the position of power, self-disclosure may also become a way of normalizing client struggles. It is very helpful for clients to know that many family problems are more common than they realize, and they are frequently empowered by hearing about therapists' own struggles in these areas. Of course, the appropriateness and timing of self-disclosure and how these potentially powerful messages to clients should be managed should be part of the self of the therapists' conversation.

Self of the Therapist

The second-order cybernetic perspective encourages therapists' awareness of the interpersonal issues they bring into their work. Aponte (1992, 1994; Aponte & Winter, 1987) has made great effort to bring "person of the therapist" issues to the forefront of family therapy training and supervision. Aponte has developed a person/practice model (Aponte & Winter, 1987) of training that pays close attention to the need for increased therapist self-knowledge. Aponte (1994) states that the goals of the model are to lead therapists in: "(a) identifying and interpreting themes in their histories and current relationships; (b) emotionally accessing their own personal struggles, past and present; (c) articulating how they have succeeded and failed with their personal and family issues; and (d) making their own personal values, philosophy, and social factors explicit for themselves" (p. 4). Since this is an important part of the self of the therapist growth, therapists are strongly encouraged to seek their own personal therapy. Therapists' greater awareness of personal issue is a growing expectation in the field for all therapists who are bringing themselves into client systems and influencing these systems based on their own interpersonal histories. The following case may help make many of these ideas more clear and relevant in working with Muslim families.

Case Example

The Ibrahims are a middle-class family from Egypt. Asra and Naser have been married for 19 years, the first marriage for him and the second for her. Asma and Naser have two children, Nasim, 16, and Musa, 14. Naser has worked as an engineer in the oil industry all of his adult life. Asra is a full-time homemaker. Asra sought therapy because of the increased distance and conflict between Nasim and Naser. A main incident that made them come to therapy was that Asra gave permission to Nasim to go on a short trip with a friend without consulting with him, and when he found out and called her daughter to come home, she refused, and Asra supported her daughter's decision.

Naser attended therapy reluctantly and cautiously, stating in the first session that he was "not sure how women could possibly understand me" and that he expected to be "condemned and blamed" for what was happening between him and his daughter. He was more concerned about Nasim and wanted to learn ways to be a better father to her but was not interested in working on his marriage, which he considered unlikely to change. He believed that the marital problems were rooted in Asra's abusive relationship with her ex-husband and believed that her history set her up to "reject and distrust men," dooming his efforts at intimacy with failure. Nasim, an attractive and energetic 16-year-old, agreed to come to therapy reluctantly and voiced her annoyances and frustrations about her mother's continuing attempts to get her to talk about her feelings, her relationship with her father, and her parents' marriage, about which she reported hearing their complaints for many years. Nasim was using the same words that her mother was using to describe the conflict she had with her father, which seemed to indicate a mother-daughter coalition against the father.

I used many ways of creating dialogue between family members around the meaning of each family member's behavior. Asra believed that Naser wanted to have control over her and Nasim but allow their son, Musa, to make his own decisions, so his behavior to her meant that he liked to be the patriarch of the family and control women. Nasim believed that her father's way of thinking was backward and traditional and that he could not possibly understand how his way of thinking was impacting her way of responding and behaving. Musa believed that while his father had good intentions and loved his children, he was at times very unreasonable and controlling, especially towards his sister and mother, but Musa had split loyalties to all of them and didn't want to be caught in the middle. Naser felt very isolated and excluded from knowing many things that were shared between his wife and his children and felt that their behavior not only meant lack of respect but that his loving intentions were also not valued and appreciated.

In our family therapy sessions we worked around belief systems regarding gender roles and patriarchal cultural practices that trap both men and women in conflictual relationships, but I tried to honor their family values and belief systems as well. In post-modern therapy, the intent is to engage family members in a dialogue rather than assume a position of authority, expertise, and knowledge about the family values, individual roles, or cultural discourses. This model is sensitive to cultural discourses and believes that therapy takes place within this setting. Therapy and its environment cannot be separated. My goal in this case was not to expect them to take on my values. It was intended to help the family members discuss, explore, and clarify values that were important to them. Gender roles and values were discussed because it was part of their primary concern and created a common language for all of them to understand the problem. I was able to convince Asra to consider the impact of the previous abusive relationship on her current relationship and try to separate her emotional reactions in each relationship. Asra was also able to have more sympathy for Naser's loneliness in the family and admitted that she never thought about it in this way. Naser had a better understanding of the power dynamics and how his wife and daughter perceived him. Nasim and Musa were able to have a better understanding of their parents' struggles and asked for better boundaries between themselves as a siblings' subsystem and their parents' subsystem. At the end of therapy, the family members were more comfortable with each other, and the issues they were struggling with shifted from mistrust and disconnections to raising successful children, collaboration, and trust. These issues appeared more 'normal' and more manageable to them. They decided what they wanted consultation on, when they needed it, and when they no longer needed it.

Summary

Post-modern family therapy attempts to provide a psychologically safe space and process where people can freely contribute to the conversation and influence its direction and outcome. They are invited to connect, collaborate, and construct with each other and the therapists towards newness or simply the possibilities of newness and transformation of thoughts, feelings, emotions, and actions. There is also transformation in relationships or, put differently, inherent in new forms of conversations or new forms of relationships. People begin to think about and experience each other and themselves differently; therefore, their relationships with each other change.

Each person is an integral part of the conversational process and its dynamic, complex web of interchanges. No one person can be identified as the source of newness. The process enhances self-agency because each person has a sense of authorship, self-competency, and responsibility for the therapy and for the future. Each participant's circumstances are distinct, and each course of therapy is novel. The way each therapeutic experience transfers outside the therapy room is often unique and creates relationship shifts. Interestingly, clients often report that between consultations changes in their thinking and interactions occur that they often view as permanent changes. In this fashion, post-modern therapy can be viewed as a context for new possibilities within families. It seems obvious that systemic therapy is inevitably connected to modernism. Nevertheless, therapists and clients have tremendously benefited from post-modernism perspectives and can use it creatively in working with Muslim families.

REFERENCES

Anderson, H. (1997). *Conversation, language, and possibilities: A postmodern approach to therapy*. New York: Basic Books.

Anderson, H., & Goolishian, H. (1988). Human systems as linguistic systems. *Family Process, 27*, 371-393.

Anderson, H., & Goolishian, H. (1992). The client as the expert: A not knowing approach to therapy. In S. McNee & K. Gergen (Eds.), *Therapy as a social construction* (pp. 25-39). London: Sage Publications.

Anderson, W.T. (1990). *Reality isn't what it used to be*. New York: Harper & Row.

Aponte, H. (1992). Training the person of the therapist in structural family therapy. *Journal of Marital and Family Therapy, 18*, 269-281.

Aponte, H. (1994). How personal can training get. *Journal of Marital and Family Therapy, 1*, 3-15.

Aponte, H., & Winter, J. (1987). The person and practice of the therapist: Treatment and training. *Journal of Psychotherapy and the Family, 20*, 85-111.

Derrida, J. (1976). *Of grammatology*. Baltimore: Johns Hopkins University Press.

Gergen, K. (1991). *The saturated self*. New York: Basic Books.

Hoffman, L. (1985). Beyond power and control: Towards a "second-order" family systems therapy. *Family Systems Medicine, 3*, 381-396.

Hoffman, L. (1990). Constructing realities: An art of lenses. *Family Process, 20*, 1-13.

Hoffman, L. (1993). *Exchanging voices*. London: Karnac.

Lyotard, J.F. (1984). *The postmodern condition: A report on knowledge*. Manchester: Manchester University Press.

Maturana, H., & Varela, F. (1984). *The tree of knowledge: Biological roots of human understanding*. London: Shambhala.

Mills, S.D., & Sprenkle, D.H. (1995). Family therapy in the postmodern era. *Family Relations, 44*, 368-376.

Parry, A. (1991). A universe of stories. *Family Process, 30*, 37-54.

Satir, V. (1964). *Conjoint family therapy*. Palo Alto: Science and Behavior Books.
Saussure, F. (1959). *Course in general linguistics*. London: Collins.
Von Glasersfeld, G. (1984). An introduction to radical constructivism. In P. Watzlawick (Ed.), *The invented reality* (pp. 17–40). New York: Norton.
Whitaker, C.A., & Bumberry, W.M. (1988). *Dancing with the family: A symbolic-experiential approach*. New York: Brunner/Mazel.

CONCLUSION

Family therapy theories have shown to be valuable tools to help mental health professionals deal a wide range of child-focused problems, couples' relational issues, sexual and intimacy issues, anxiety, depression, and psychotic disorders, as well as chemical dependency issues (Carr, 2000a, 2000b). Many family-based effective interventions have used one-size-fits-all cognitive-behavioral, psychoeducational, and psychotherapy approaches. However, my intention in writing this book was to incorporate structural, Bowenian, experiential, narrative, contextual, feminist, and post-modern family therapy models for providing culturally sensitive interventions to Muslim families. The theories and clinical cases covered in this book are based on 20 years of teaching, research, and practice and can be very useful for training students and for clinical practice. Family therapists working with Muslim families may benefit from incorporating essential elements of these effective family therapy theories and family-based treatments into their own style of practice.

Further, while the family therapy approaches covered in this book have shown great effectiveness in my work with Muslim families, Sprenkle, Davis, and Lebow (2009) discuss common factors and change instruments that make most forms of psychotherapy and family therapy achieve their goals, irrespective of therapists' theoretical orientations or their use of specific techniques. There are empirical evidence that some of these common factors include the therapeutic relationship, client personality, therapist personality, and expectation and optimism of the client and the therapist (Sprenkle, Davis, & Lebow, 2009).

Effective therapists providing marital and family therapy to Muslim families are those who develop a connecting and compassionate relationship with clients (Daneshpour, 1998). The main factors for clients' change are inspiration and having incentive to participate in treatment as well as willingness and readiness to change (Daneshpour, 1998). There are many factors common to most good therapists, such as being well adjusted themselves, being capable of adjusting their expectations to clients' prospects and preference, being creative in finding innovative ways to articulate clients' struggles and challenges, and offering clients convincing rationales for acquiring new skills for problem solving.

Moreover, most forms of family therapy help family members develop adaptive behaviors, foster healthy thinking patterns, learn to regulate feelings, and make healthy emotional connections. The common factors that are distinctly unique to systemic family therapy and differentiate it from individual models of psychotherapy are: viewing problems within the context of relational patterns; always taking the family and social system of the individual into consideration in therapy; and working hard to develop a therapeutic relationship with all members of the family and their social network.

Further, practitioners who work with clients of Muslim descent both in the East and the West should expect to encounter some emotional, cognitive, and behavioral styles that are impacted by the religion of Islam, the collectivistic cultural backgrounds of Muslim families, both colonial and postcolonial politics, and some unique gender dynamics. Of course, like any other group, not all Muslims are alike; they are spread along a continuum from traditional to progressive. Along this continuum, the two portions of each perspective make the cultural differences between the clients. Thus, we can conclude that the more traditional a client, the more his identity is collective.

This traditional versus progressive characteristic of Muslim families should be considered only as an intellectual framework that therapists could use to understand a specific Muslim family's dynamics. Obviously, the responsibility lies with the therapist to recognize the unique characteristics of each family and place them on a traditional/progressive cultural map. These maps are not the only representative of clients' reality, but they can be used as a framework by which practitioners understand the reality of the clients' lived experiences and provide appropriate therapeutic services.

Based on the shared cultural characteristics of Muslim families and the family therapy theories presented in this book, I recommend that therapists use a culturally sensitive approach revising widely held notions about individuation, independence, and a rigid and one-dimensional view of Muslim family dynamics.

A culturally sensitive approach in family therapy is very important in this era of globalization, when Western cultural values are often used as the definitive choice for all people, regardless of their heritage or culture. Family therapists have great responsibility to use family theories in working with Muslim families so they can develop a better understanding of their family dynamics. This perspective will promote greater understanding, respect, and compassion for Muslim families' relational realties and will promote diversity and pluralism within this era of globalization.

References

Carr, A. (2000a). Research update: Evidence based practice in family therapy and systemic consultation, I. Child focused problems. *Journal of Family Therapy, 22,* 29–59.

Carr, A. (2000b). Research update: Evidence based practice in family therapy and systemic consultation. II. Adult focused problems. *Journal of Family Therapy, 22,* 273–295.

Daneshpour, M. (1998). Muslim families and family therapy. *Journal of Marriage and Family Therapy, 24,* 287–300. doi: 10.1111/j.1752-0606.1998.tb01090.x

Sprenkle, D. H., Davis, S. D., & Lebow, J. L. (2009). *Common factors in couple and family therapy: The overlooked foundation for effective practice.* New York: Guilford Press.

INDEX

Note: Page numbers in italics indicate figures and tables.